WRITERS AND THEIR WORK

ISOBEL ARMSTRONG
General Editor

SAMUEL BECKETT

SAMUEL BECKETT
Photograph of Beckett in Paris, December 1985

© John Minihan

SAMUEL BECKETT

Sinéad Mooney

NORTHCOTE
BRITISH
COUNCIL

For Ian

© Copyright 2005 by Sinéad Mooney

First published in 2005 by Northcote House Publishers Ltd, Horndon, Tavistock, Devon, PL19 9NQ, United Kingdom.
Tel: +44 (01822) 810066. Fax: +44 (01822) 810034.

British Library Cataloguing-in-Publication Data
A catalogue record for this book is available from the British Library

ISBN 978-0-7463-0857-8 paperback

Typeset by TW Typesetting, Plymouth, Devon
Printed and bound in the United Kingdom

Contents

Acknowledgements

I would like to thank the Department of English of the National University of Ireland, Galway for an understanding distribution of my teaching, which allowed me to complete this project. My Beckett seminar students of the academic year 2003/4 also deserve honourable mention. My thanks are also due to Steven Connor for suggesting I undertook this book, and for his encouragement over the past few years. Hilary Walford's thoughtful copy-editing has earned my gratitude. My love and thanks as ever to Ian Flanagan for innumerable discussions of Beckett, and for simply being there. Finally, Beckett's writings are quoted by permission of the Beckett Estate, Faber & Faber Ltd and the Calder Educational Trust in the UK, and Grove Press in the USA.

Biographical Outline

As Beckett wrote so many individually published works in English and French, only a selection is listed here. A complete list is given in the Bibliography. Unless otherwise specified, dates given here are for the first production of plays and first publication of fiction and poetry.

1906   Samuel Barclay Beckett born Good Friday, 13 April, in affluent suburb of Foxrock, County Dublin. Elder brother Frank born 1902. Father William (Bill) worked as quantity surveyor in Dublin, mother (May) had been a nurse before her marriage. Ancestors on both sides pillars of Dublin Protestant establishment.

1920   Follows his brother to Portora Royal School, Enniskillen, Northern Ireland.

1923   Attends Trinity College Dublin to study Modern Languages.

1927   Awarded his BA degree, winning the Gold medal for coming first in the First Class. Accepts temporary teaching post at Campbell College, Belfast.

1928   Begins to lecture at the École Normale Supérieure in Paris as part of its exchange programme with TCD. Meets Irish poet Thomas MacGreevy, and through him James Joyce and his circle. First of many visits to Germany to stay with his cousin Peggy Sinclair and her family in Kassel.

1929   Publication of first commission, an essay on Joyce's *Work in Progress*, 'Dante ... Bruno . Vico .. Joyce' and his first short story 'Assumption' in the journal *transition*.

1930   First independently published work, *Whoroscope*, wins the £10 prize in a poetry competition sponsored by Nancy Cunard's Hours Press. Rift with Joyce after Beckett rejects the advances of Lucia Joyce, who is already showing signs of mental disturbance. Returns to Dublin to take up lectureship at TCD.

1931   *Proust* published.

1932   Resigns from TCD and returns to Paris. Writes *Dream of Fair to Middling Women*, published posthumously in 1992. 'Dante and the Lobster' appears in *This Quarter*. Returns to Dublin.

1933   Health worsens. Deaths of SB's father and his cousin Peggy Sinclair.

1934   Leaves Dublin for London for psychoanalysis with Dr Wilfred Bion at Tavistock Clinic, which lasts till end of 1935. Reviews for literary magazines. Publication of *More Pricks Than Kicks*.

1935   Publication of collection of poems, *Echo's Bones and Other Precipitates*. Attends one of Jung's Tavistock lectures. *Murphy* begun.

1936   Travels in Germany September 1936–April 1937.

1937   Leaves Dublin for Paris, which he regards from now on as his permanent home. Testifies as witness in Oliver St John Gogarty libel case on behalf of his cousins the Sinclairs. Brief love affair with Peggy Guggenheim.

1937–8 Beckett stabbed by pimp in Paris street. Lifelong relationship with Suzanne Deschevaux-Dumesnil begins. Publication of *Murphy*. Begins to write poetry in French.

1940   Flees Paris for Vichy on German invasion. Returns to occupied Paris and becomes involved in Resistance cell Gloria SMH.

1941–2 Gloria SMH betrayed. Beckett escapes with Suzanne to the village of Roussillon in Vichy France.

1942–5 In Roussillon, writes *Watt*, his last work in English for some time.

1945   After liberation of Rousillon, Beckett returns to Paris, visits his family in Dublin, and works in Saint-Lô in Normandy as a member of an Irish Red Cross

	team. Awarded the Croix de Guerre for his Resistance work.
1946–52	The period known as the 'siege in the room'. Begins to write prose and drama in French.
1946	Writes his first novel in French, *Mercier et Camier*, and four novellas, 'Premier amour', 'L'Expulsé', 'Le Calmant' and 'Le Fin'.
1947	Writes his first play in French, *Eleuthéria* (published posthumously), and the first novel of what would become the Trilogy, *Molloy*.
1948	Writes the second Trilogy novel, *Malone meurt*, and begins *En attendant Godot*.
1949	Completes *En attendant Godot* and begins final Trilogy novel, *L'Innommable*.
1950	Completes *L'Innommable* and begins *Textes pour rien*. Death of May Beckett.
1951	*Molloy* and *Malone meurt* published.
1952	*En attendant Godot* published. With a legacy from his mother, buys land and builds a house at Ussy-sur-Marne, which becomes his preferred location for writing.
1953	*En attendant Godot* produced in Paris at the Théâtre de Babylone, with Roger Blin directing. *Watt* published. Begins to translate *Godot* into English. *L'Innommable* published.
1954	Death of Frank Beckett.
1955	First London production of *Waiting for Godot*. *Nouvelles et textes pour rien* published. *Molloy* published in English by Olympia Press, Paris.
1956	First American production of *Waiting for Godot*. *Malone Dies* published. First English publication of *Godot*.
1957	*Fin de partie* published, produced in French in London, and translated into English as *Endgame*. *All That Fall*, Beckett's first radio play, produced by the BBC.
1958	Writes *Krapp's Last Tape*, which is produced at the Royal Court, London. *Endgame* published and produced in London, and *The Unnamable* published.
1959	Awarded honorary D.Litt. by TCD. *Embers* written and broadcast on BBC.

1960 Shares Prix International des Éditeurs with Jorge Luis Borges. Moves to the Boulevard St Jacques, which would remain his Paris home for the rest of his life.

1961–2 Marries Suzanne Deschevaux-Dumesnil in Folkestone. *Happy Days* produced in New York. Writes *Words and Music* and *Cascando* (in French). *Words and Music* is broadcast on the BBC.

1963 Writes *Film*. Beckett assists with the German production of *Play* in Ulm-Donau, and from this point on is almost invariably closely associated with the major productions of his plays. *Cascando* broadcast in French on RTF.

1964 Only visit to America, to be present at the making of *Film*. *Play* produced in English at the Old Vic, London. *How It Is* published.

1965 Writes his first television play, *Eh Joe*, broadcast by the BBC the following year. *Film* shown at the New York Film Festival. *Imagination Dead Imagine* published.

1967 *No's Knife: Collected Shorter Prose 1945–1966* (containing all the novellas but 'Premier amour', *Texts for Nothing*, *From an Abandoned Work* and *Residua*) published.

1969 Wins Nobel Prize for Literature. *Breath* produced at the Eden Theatre, New York.

1972 *Not I* produced at the Lincoln Centre, New York. *The Lost Ones* published.

1975–6 *That Time* and *Footfalls* written and performed at the Royal Court. *For to End Yet Again and Other Fizzles* and *All Strange Away* published. *Ghost Trio* published.

1977 *Ghost Trio, . . . but the clouds . . .* and the television version of *Not I* broadcast on BBC2.

1978 *Six Residua* published.

1980 *A Piece of Monologue* produced in New York. *Company* published.

1981 *Rockaby* produced in Buffalo, New York. *Ohio Impromptu* produced at Ohio State University. *Ill Seen Ill Said* published.

1982 *Quad* broadcast in Germany by Süddeutscher Rundfunk and later in year by BBC. *Catastrophe* (French)

	produced at the Avignon Festival. *Ill Seen Ill Said* published.
1983	*Nacht und Träume* broadcast by Süddeutscher Rundfunk. *Worstward Ho* published.
1984	*Collected Poems 1930–1978* and *Collected Shorter Plays* published.
1988	*Stirrings Still* and *Collected Shorter Prose 1945–1980* published.
1989	Suzanne Beckett dies 17 April. Beckett dies 22 December. *Nohow On (Company, Ill Seen Ill Said, Worstward Ho)* published.

Abbreviations

C.	*Company* (New York: Grove Press, 1980)
CDW	*Samuel Beckett: The Complete Dramatic Works* (London and Boston: Faber & Faber, 1990)
CSP	*Samuel Beckett: The Complete Short Prose 1929–1989*, ed. S.E. Gontarski (New York: Grove Press, 1995)
D.	*Disjecta: Miscellaneous Writings and a Dramatic Fragment*, ed. Ruby Cohn (London: John Calder, 1983)
DFM	*Dream of Fair to Middling Women*, ed. Eoin O'Brien and Edith Fournier (Dublin: Black Cat Press, 1992)
HII	*How It Is* (London: John Calder, 1964)
ISIS	*Ill Seen Ill Said* (New York: Grove Press, 1981)
M.	*Murphy* (London: Pan, 1973)
MC	*Mercier and Camier* (London: Calder and Boyars, 1974)
MPTK	*More Pricks Than Kicks* (London: Calder & Boyars, 1970)
PTD	*Proust and Three Dialogues with Georges Duthuit* (London: John Calder, 1965)
T.	*The Beckett Trilogy: Molloy, Malone Dies, The Unnamable* (London: Pan, 1979)
W.	*Watt* (London: John Calder, 1970)
WH	*Worstward Ho* (London: John Calder, 1983)

Note on the Text

Beckett wrote virtually all his work in both French and English. However, an account of the often complex interrelation between different versions of a text during the to-and-fro of self-translation is beyond the scope of this study, which will refer only to the English texts. Below are listed alphabetically the titles of all Beckett texts referred to, with their French equivalent. Note that in a few cases no equivalent exists. For further details, see the Biographical Outline and Bibliography.

English	French
All Strange Away	
All That Fall	*Tous ceux qui tombent*
Breath	*Souffle*
. . . but the clouds . . .	*. . . que nuages . . .*
Cascando	*Cascando*
Catastrophe	*Catastrophe*
Come and Go	*Va et vient*
Company	*Compagnie*
Dream of Fair to Middling Women	
Eh Joe	*Hé Joe*
	Eleuthéria
Embers	*Cendres*
Endgame	*Fin de partie*
Enough	*Assez*
Film	*Film*
Footfalls	*Pas*
From an Abandoned Work	*D'un ouvrage abandonné*

Ghost Trio	Trio du fantôme
Happy Days	Oh les beaux jours
How It Is	Comment c'est
Imagination Dead Imagine	Imagination morte imaginez
Ill Seen Ill Said	Mal vu mal dit
Krapp's Last Tape	La dernière bande
Lessness	Sans
The Lost Ones	Le Dépeupleur
Malone Dies	Malone meurt
Molloy	Molloy
More Pricks Than Kicks	
Murphy	Murphy
Nacht und Träume	Nacht und Träume
Not I	Pas moi
Ohio Impromptu	L'Impromptu d'Ohio
A Piece of Monologue	Solo
Ping	Bing
Play	Comédie
Proust	Proust
Quad	Quad
Rockaby	Berceuse
Rough for Radio I and II	Esquisse radiophonique; Pochade radiophonique
Still	Immobile
Texts for Nothing	Textes pour rien
That Time	Cette fois
The Calmative	Le Calmant
The End	Le Fin
The Expelled	L'Expulsé
Three Dialogues with Georges Duthuit	
The Unnamable	L'Innommable
Waiting for Godot	En attendant Godot
Watt	Watt
What Where	Quoi où
Words and Music	Paroles et Musique
Worstward Ho	

Prologue

'Habit is a great deadener', remarks Vladimir in *Waiting for Godot (CDW* 84). Certainly, since the success of *Waiting for Godot* in 1953, Beckett's disintegrating world of dotards and vagrants, his relentless formal innovations, the insistent surrealism of his stage images, and his moves between high formality and low farce, have attained a certain familiarity. Hailed successively as existentialist, dramatist of the Absurd, modernist, postmodernist – to mention only the most commonly applied labels – his writing in all genres has been encircled, arguably deadened, with almost unprecedented amounts of critical commentary. The sheer weight of criticism his work has attracted offers an ironic contrast to the œuvre of a writer who has for preference embraced uncertainty and impotence as his arena of aesthetic endeavour. In a rare interview in 1956, Beckett marked off his terrain from that of his revered James Joyce, commenting that, whereas Joyce was a 'superb manipulator of material [. . .] making words do the absolute maximum of work', he himself has chosen the opposite route: 'the kind of work I do is one in which I'm not master of my material [. . .] I'm working with ignorance, impotence.'¹ This statement, the closest Beckett ever came to a credo, would hold good for the succeeding decades of his writing life, through successive experiments in the 'weakening' of conventional narrative and dramatic syntax. Even the single most audacious act of his career, his decision to eschew his native language for French, was performed in a spirit of deliberate self-impoverishment.

Thus, there is often a gulf between Beckett's work and critical interpretations of it. Confident declarations of meaning appear almost comically inappropriate in relation to a body of

1

writing in which everything is contingent and provisional, where the most definitive word is, as Beckett said of *Godot*, 'perhaps'.[2] Critical readings of Beckett necessarily involve a 'tidying' of a deliberately untidy œuvre, a suppression of the carnivalesque uncertainty of Beckett's career-long 'perhaps', with its undermining of absolute truths and certainties, and dissolution of the abstract and systematizing forces of rationality. Straddling French and English, blurring generic boundaries, his style is characterized by comic false starts, digressions and irregularities, continually resisting being drawn into a single comprehensive thesis or system. It is difficult, therefore, for academic forms and approaches to negotiate Beckett's world without imposing artificial modes of order. Yet it is also curiously compelling. Despite the fact that the critic regularly receives short shrift throughout Beckett's writing ('Crritic!' is, famously, the worst insult Estragon can throw at Vladimir in *Waiting for Godot*, to mention only one instance), it is an œuvre that compels the reader or spectator into the same position as its succession of ruined thinkers and seekers after knowledge.

As Beckett's creatures never entirely give up worrying at the possibility of meaning, neither can the reader. If Beckett is finally more modernist than postmodernist, it is because his shattered world retains at its centre a void whose shape remains hauntingly meaningful. Likewise, things resist the processes of signification in Beckett's work because meaning has leached away, not because it was never there, much in the same manner as subjectivity is a befuddled memory, and the body a disintegrating hulk. If confusion rather than certainty is what characterizes Beckett's work, it never amounts to a simple abandonment of the pursuit of knowledge. Meaning, or the possibility of meaningfulness, remains to haunt Beckett's writing, even if it is as nightmare rather than redemption, as when *Endgame*'s Hamm voices a suspicion as to whether he and Clov are 'not beginning to . . . to . . . mean something?' (*CDW* 108). Similarly, if Beckett's work enacts the collapse of the metaphysical certainties that have long sustained Western thought – belief in a God, in the unity of the self and the knowability of experience, the capacity of language to communicate – then it does so semi-regretfully, like his early

2

anti-hero Murphy walking 'round and round cathedrals that it was too late to enter' (*M*. 46).

Furthermore, even in works like the mature stage plays, which actively resist the imposition of systematic meaning, Beckett counterpoints their visions of irrational shapelessness and purposelessness with austere dramatic structures of repetitions, parallels and patternings. Beckett's work straddles the paradox of attempting to dismantle the rational from within, and to use words to express inexpressibility; in this it frequently sets up the signs of meaning and immediately cancels them, kicking the interpretative stool out from under the reader. Even if the effect is frequently blackly comic, our amusement at the predicaments of Beckett's impotent tramps and clowns is unsettled, as their dilemmas are ours also; patterns of coherence are formulated and then continually dissolved before the eyes of the reader and spectator.

Yet neither does Beckett's world constitute a universe determinate enough to be properly tragic, despite its capacity for being read in symbolic, universal terms; his cast of bungling anti-heroes, cripples and freaks continually glance off tragedy into low farce, cerebral games and ritual, or lose themselves along the slippages of language. Rather, his writing in all genres seems to partake of something of the governing metaphor of his most famous play, that of the indeterminate yet curiously suggestive act of waiting. The state of being suspended – between acting and not acting, meaning and meaninglessness, shape and chaos, the black comedy of the decaying body or senescent mind and the bleakly universal philosophical vision, between the impossibility of expression and the necessity to go on speaking – is a particularly useful state of being for an artist whose universe is fundamentally ambiguous.

3

1

'Difficult music': The Early Fiction

Beckett believed at the end of his life that 1945 and 1946 were the years in which his apprenticeship ended, and in which he experienced the recognition that would condition his subsequent development as a writer. Certainly, the plotless, placeless post-war monologues and drama written in French stand out sharply from the experimental English fiction of the pre-war period. Despite Beckett's perennial suspicion of what he calls in his Joyce essay 'Dante . . . Bruno . Vico . . Joyce' the danger of the 'neatness of identifications' (*D*. 19), the division of his career into pre- and post-1945–6 is one he held to. 'All that goes before forget', admonishes the opening sentence of the much later short story *Enough*, as so many of Beckett's mature works do, explicitly or implicitly asking the reader to disregard previous work. Yet the Beckett reader cannot ignore the almost two decades of writing in English that precede the writing of *Molloy* in mid-1947, in which Beckett experimented in a dizzying variety of modes, registers and genres, which, if they often threaten to collapse under their own weight, or are scarred by incommensurate impulses, nonetheless show Beckett struggling to find 'a kind of knowledge which would permit me to act', in the full knowledge that 'perhaps there are only wrong tracks'.[1]

MORE PRICKS THAN KICKS AND *DREAM OF FAIR TO MIDDLING WOMEN*

From the start of his career, Beckett absorbed the modernist dictum to 'make it new': the exhaustion of realism, the need

4

for innovation, and the concomitant need continually to re-create form and language within each new work. This insistently innovative framework was already in place even before Beckett began to write fiction. His early criticism – particularly his self-defining essays on Joyce and Proust – while of only intermittent value for its insights on its ostensible subjects, shows a precocious and scholarly young essayist honing his own radical ideas on two masters, before beginning to carry them out in his own early writing. His first published work, the essay 'Dante . . . Bruno . Vico . . Joyce' (1929) is a self-consciously learned defence of Joyce's *Finnegans Wake* (in 1929 still incomplete and known by its working title of 'Work in Progress'). In defending Joyce's experimentalism from an implied reader's hostility, Beckett preaches the need to reinvigorate an overly 'sophisticated' English he perceives as in danger of being 'abstracted to death' (*D*. 28) by a new writing that will 'recognise the importance of treating words as something more than polite symbols' (*D*. 28). Joyce, who has 'desophisticated language', has arrived, according to Beckett, at 'direct expression', a 'savage economy of hieroglyphics', a form of writing in which 'form *is* content, content *is* form' and in which writing 'is not *about* something' but '*that something itself*' (*D*. 27–8).

In this press of heartfelt italics, the young Beckett arrives at a kind of early manifesto; literature must not be skimmed for the 'scant cream of sense', for content at the expense of form, but form and content must be inextricably fused. In Beckett's early fiction, this urgent experimentalism manifests itself as a self-conscious and frequently shrill literary exhibitionism. It is hardly surprising the earliest writings found little success, or that Beckett withheld permission for a reprint of *More Pricks Than Kicks* until 1970, while the long-unpublished novel that provided much of the material for that collection saw the light of day only after Beckett's death.

Beckett's first novel, the unfinished *Dream of Fair to Middling Women*, was written in 1932 in Paris, when he was 26, but, having made the round of publishers unsuccessfully, remained unpublished until 1992. At the time of its writing, its author's published work consisted of a prize-winning poem, *Whoroscope*, his critical essay 'Dante . . . Bruno . Vico . . Joyce' (1929)

5

and the monograph *Proust* (1931), and several poems and short prose texts, some of which were incorporated in *Dream*. By the time of the novel's posthumous publication sixty years later, Beckett's worldwide reputation ensured intense critical interest, and *Dream* has remained primarily a mine for Beckett scholars seeking insights into his artistic apprenticeship. As what Beckett, looking back on *Dream* towards the end of his life, dubbed 'the chest into which I threw my wild thoughts',[2] *Dream* is a literary curiosity unlikely to be of interest to anyone other than the Beckett specialist, scuppered as it is by florid over-writing and affected intellectual gymnastics. Loosely based around the life and loves of a young bohemian, Belacqua Shuah, the novel is aptly summed up by John Pilling as 'a pot-pourri of irreconcilable elements, part-autobiography, part-fiction and part looseleaf folder for any passing expressive gesture'.[3] Certainly, it is more nakedly and anxiously autobiographical than any of Beckett's writing would ever be again. At times it approaches a *roman-à-clef*, incorporating thinly disguised portraits of relatives and friends, including his cousin, Peggy Sinclair, and her parents, Professor Thomas Rudmose-Brown of Trinity College, and James Joyce's daughter, Lucia.

Dream's tone is frequently furiously choleric, scrambling desperately between registers and languages, the narrative appearing to wish to cast itself out of its 'native' English and into Latin, Italian, French or German, all of which combine on the page – sometimes within the same sentence – to form an at times unreadable linguistic turmoil. Its tenuous picaresque plot consists chiefly of Belacqua's encounters with a series of grotesque women, the Smeraldina-Rima, the Syra-Cusa, the Fricas, mother and daughter, the Alba, and a cartoonish supporting cast of assorted minor poets and literary hangers-on. Any semblance of plot is frequently overwhelmed by lengthy digressions and detachable set pieces that attempt to forge an aesthetic elaborating on his contention that 'form *is* content, content *is* form':

> The experience of my reader shall be between the phrases, in the silence, communicated by the intervals, not the terms, of the statement, between the flowers that cannot coexist, the antithetical (nothing so simple as antithetical) seasons of words, his experience

shall be the menace, the miracle, the memory, of an unspeakable trajectory. (*DFM* 137)

At its best, *Dream* achieves a kind of virtuosic frenzy, combining hectic word-coining and dizzying linguistic play with a determination to roam free of the constraints of conventional form. At worst, it is florid, affected and self-congratulating, larded with a scholarship that, while considerable, is primarily a proudly-brandished badge of allegiance to the avant-garde.

As well as being a repository for earlier writings – the poems 'Enueg I', 'Alba', 'Dortmunder' and 'Casket of Pralinen for a Daughter of a Dissipated Mandarin' – substantial sections of *Dream of Fair to Middling Women* also appear almost verbatim in the 1934 short story collection *More Pricks Than Kicks*. 'The Smeraldina's Billet Doux', 'A Wet Night' and 'Ding-Dong' are all quarried from *Dream*. Despite its self-consciously scandalous title, taken from the words of the divine vision experienced by Paul on the road to Damascus in the New Testament,[4] *More Pricks Than Kicks* is a rather more decorous affair than *Dream*. The furiously choleric tone of *Dream* has muted into one of more even comical archness; the incessant disruption of narrative perspective has settled into a more settled narratorial stance. The collection of ten interlinked stories effects in essence a compromise between its author's desire for experimentalism and parody, and the more traditional imperatives of plot and character.

More Pricks Than Kicks shares with *Dream* its hero, the feckless Dubliner Belacqua Shuah, whose unlikely name and characteristic indolence Beckett borrowed from the slothful lutemaker of Canto 4 of Dante's *Purgatorio*, who is doomed to linger after death under a rock at the portals of Purgatory for his laziness in repenting his sins. Already, this first Beckett anti-hero contains important elements of his successors; he combines the clown and the scholar, suffers from the 'ruined' feet and 'spavined gait' that signal the psychological as well as physical collapse of Beckett's protagonists, and is the prototype of the solipsistic Beckett male whose ability to confront and delimit reality is conspicuously deficient. The stories partake in this inability, refusing to tidy a reality their narrator perceives as incoherent into neat categories, an activity Beckett refers to

7

disdainfully in his *Three Dialogues with George Duthuit* as mere 'good housekeeping' (*PTD* 125). At the same time, however, they do not swerve away from conventional forms as violently and incessantly as *Dream*. Much as the book cannot seem to decide whether it is a semi-congruent collection of stories or a series of episodes that cannot quite cohere into a novel, *More Pricks Than Kicks* hovers between convention and carnival, form and formlessness, with its narrator generally quiescent to the obligations of traditional form, though indicating at frequent intervals how arbitrary and irksome he finds them.

More Pricks Than Kicks opens with the death of a lobster and concludes with the death and obsequies of the collection's protagonist, having journeyed through manifold fiascos in the interim. By far the strongest story in the collection is the opening 'Dante and the Lobster', in which the seedy protagonist, having mused on Dante's depiction of damnation, observes with horror the boiling alive of a lobster. Exposed 'cruciform on the oilcloth' (*MPTK* 21) as the scapegoat for the impersonal and horrifying forces of human and divine 'justice', it becomes the displaced focus of a pity seldom explicitly extended to human beings at this stage in Beckett's work. While Belacqua tries to console himself with a platitude – 'Well [. . .] it's a quick death, God help us all' (*MPTK* 21) – the final words of the story, which apparently come out of nowhere, contradict this, in a final appalled acknowledgement of suffering that looks ahead to his mature writing.

The following nine stories retreat somewhat from this nakedness of stance, and circulate more arbitrarily between the poles of love and death, *la mort* and *l'amour*, seen as analogous. Such semblances of plot as these stories possess is provided by the manner in which Belacqua's glum solipsism is continually broken down by a succession of grotesque women, often misogynistically depicted as rampantly and exclusively physical beings. Their sexual importunings prove particularly disturbing to his efforts to live quietly in his mind. The 'pricks' in the collection's title suggest less Belacqua's own quiescent 'compound of ephebe and old woman' (*MPTK* 189) than the phallic overtures of the rapacious women who try to inveigle him into union and procreation. In 'Fingal', he eludes his girlfriend in a fit of post-coital distress by pedalling furiously away on a stolen bicycle, prefiguring the bizarre eroticization of bicycles in the trilogy. In 'Love and Lethe', a suicide pact goes awry and is sidetracked into sardonically narrated al fresco sex (the 'inevitable nuptial') with one Ruby Tough, irrepressible as her name. In 'Walking Out', the disaster of sexuality and procreation is happily avoided by the crippling of Belacqua's Amazonian fiancée Lucy, so that marriage remains a non-carnal affair. In 'Yellow', while the hapless Belacqua awaits minor surgery on a neck tumour, a ludicrous sexual scenario emerges when a set of aggressive nurses grow severe upon his 'little bump of amativeness' (*MPTK* 181), before he is killed off in the story's casual conclusion. The final story, 'Draff', sees the third Mrs Shuah forming a new liaison while dressing her husband's grave.

However, these stories are ill served by a plot summary, as their most striking characteristic is narrative untidiness, particularly continual suspensions of narrative space and time, to allow for linguistically exhibitionistic asides in which verbal vividness overshadows the relatively denuded 'content' of the stories. Though less volatile and insistent than *Dream*, *More Pricks Than Kicks* continues to demonstrate Beckett's need to lambast literary norms with an armature of sophisticated weapons. While neither *Dream* nor *More Pricks Than Kicks* suggests the author would become a writer of extraordinary originality, what does shine forth from them is a genuine iconoclasm, a fierce determination to smash up anachronistic pieties and move beyond what *Dream* calls the 'chloroformed world' (*DFM* 119) of the well-made novel.

MURPHY

Murphy was written in 1935–6, and is in some sense the result of Beckett's two years in psychoanalysis with the distinguished analyst W. R. Bion at the Tavistock Clinic, London, to treat severe depression and a range of crippling psychosomatic ailments. Described on its publication in 1938 by an enthusiastic early reviewer, the novelist Kate O'Brien, as 'erudite, allusive, brilliant, impudent and rude',[5] *Murphy* has dispensed with the wilder excesses of the preceding writing. In essence,

9

it extends to the novel form the compromise between the experimental and the representational already performed in the short stories of *More Pricks Than Kicks*. The representational gift that Beckett had always possessed but seldom given rein to in his previous writing flowers into the vividly realized world of *Murphy*'s London – West Brompton, South Kensington and the suburban mental hospital Murphy regards as his personal nirvana. Much attention is devoted to its comically busy intrigues and chronological precision, even if the novel is primarily obedient to conventional novelistic rules in order to better expose them.

It has not, for instance, dispensed with third-person narration, and retains, albeit self-consciously, certain conventions of the comic novel and *Bildungsroman*, tracing as it does its hero's intellectual progress and adventures. *Murphy* does, however, represent a considerable advance on the juvenilia discussed above, bringing Beckett's literary and philosophical preoccupations together in a comic challenge to Western metaphysics from Plato onwards. Stylistically, the hectic mannerism of *More Pricks* has been refined into an elegant pedantry, unsettled with moments of pastoral pathos and diagrammatic gestures outside of language, and studded with interpolated episodes reminiscent of Sterne's *Tristram Shandy*, such as the horoscope of chapter 3 and the whole of chapter 6. It is the vitality occasioned by these competing impulses, towards and away from conventional novelistic representation, that give *Murphy* its innovativeness and playfulness.

The eponymous Murphy is a seedily solipsistic anti-hero with marked resemblances to the Belacqua of *Dream* and *More Pricks Than Kicks*. Another malcontent semi-scholar, he belongs to 'no profession or trade', lives on 'small charitable sums' and is a 'chronic emeritus' (*M*. 14, 16). A dualist drawn to the life of the mind, he avoids work, which involves the exertions of the body; instead he devotes most of his ingenuity to achieving a quietist life of self-delighting solitude and inertia. This is achieved by the remarkable method of self-bondage, quieting the body by immobilizing it with scarves in a rocking chair. In so far as the 'big world' exacts from Murphy any effort at engagement with it (besides withdrawal, his preferred one), he copes with it at one remove, via his horoscope.

10

In *Murphy*, Beckett satirizes the fiction of self-identity. Western metaphysics has defined the ideal state of Being as a timeless self-presence that is self-sufficient and self-identical, positing God as Supreme Being or Unmoved Mover existing above and beyond the human stratum of temporal flux and movement. Descartes and his followers – such as the Belgian Occasionalist philosopher Arnold Guelincx quoted in *Murphy* – draw on the belief that the intellectual dimension of the human subject is able to participate in the Divine Being. Thus it can rise above its mortal physical existence and transcend time to become absolutely at one with itself, the Cartesian *cogito* Beckett continually exposes to ridicule. Murphy in his rocking chair aspires to a divine condition of self-sufficiency, a 'Belacqua bliss'. His project is to seclude himself entirely from the outside world with its irritations of desire and human contact, to achieve total self-realization in the nirvana of the isolated ego.

However, Beckett satirically exposes the folly of this project. The whole of *Murphy*'s chapter 6, a detailed description of Murphy's mind, with an epigraph satirically rewritten to juxtapose Murphy and the metaphysical definition of God (as Love, which is sufficient unto itself), satirizes Murphy's ideal of splendid self-adequacy: 'Murphy's mind pictured itself as a large hollow sphere hermetically closed to the universe without [. . .]' (*M*. 63). He is unable to connect his body and his mind and unable to reconcile his need for self-immersed indifference with his desire for his prostitute lover, the wistful tart with a heart, Celia. When Neary tells Murphy that his 'conarium has shrunk to nothing', he is invoking one of the odder details of Descartes's philosophy, whereby the conarium or pineal gland was the means by which the otherwise obscure intercourse between mind and body is carried on. With his conarium shrunk to nothing, Murphy leads a completely dual existence, attempting to deny his body the sexual 'music' it craves and wanting to live entirely in his mind, while Celia – in the tradition of her grotesquely physical predecessors in *Dream* and *More Pricks Than Kicks* – reminds him all too tangibly of the existence of the problematic body. Thus the novel as a whole mocks the traditional metaphysical doctrine that man can be identified as a timeless, silent and immutable

11

consciousness, wittily demonstrating instead that he is in fact a corporeal being irrevocably bound to time, language and movement. The combination of Murphy's determined solipsism and Celia's pragmatic world view and more worldly ambitions for him contains both an erudite philosophical parody and the seeds of a comically incongruous situation typical of the conventional comic novel.

In contrast to the incidentless nature of the later fiction, *Murphy* has a relatively coherent, if entirely inconsequential, comic sub-plot. This involves a set of interconnected Dublin characters – the pseudo-philosophers Neary and Wylie, the lovestruck Miss Counihan and the manservant Cooper – in pursuit of Murphy for diverse reasons. The Dublin quartet, who are explicitly manipulated like puppets by the sardonic narrator, offer a diagrammatic parody of the sexual intrigues of the traditional novel. It is a 'closed system' in which libido is transferred about as arbitrarily as the counters in a game, as all the characters converge on a reluctant Murphy. This underpins in conventional fashion the primary action of Murphy's fascinated retreat into the world of the mental hospital, the Magdalen Mental Mercyseat, as he supposes its inmates to be blessedly cut off from 'the rudimentary blessings of the layman's reality' (*M.* 101), enjoying the withdrawal from the world he has always craved, so that the padded cells seem 'indoor bowers of bliss' (*M.* 103). The novel's bizarre climax occurs when Murphy attempts a game of chess with one of the 'higher schizoids' whose alienation so fascinates him, but whose chess is less a game as conventionally conceived than it is a ballet of non-engagement. Murphy (White) attempts to force Black to engage with him, to the extent of trying to give him pieces, and when this fails, attempts to play Black's game, imitating him. The game ends with the chessmen of Black (Mr Endon, his name Greek for 'within') barely disarranged from their starting position, but with Murphy's scattered in a chaos similar to the way his own body will shortly be dispersed. The end of his experiments in solipsism – blown to bits when his improvised gas heater misfires – is narrated robustly, as tragicomic catastrophe with the emphasis on the comic element. After the cremation of what remains of Murphy's body, his last wishes (to be flushed down the toilet during a performance at Dublin's Abbey Theatre) are disregarded. His ashes instead end up on the floor of a pub and are eventually 'swept away with the sand, the beer, the butts, the glass, the matches, the spits, the vomit' (M. 154). All Murphy's grandiose philosophical aspirations are reduced to ashes.

Of course, it would be inaccurate to read Murphy as a conventional novel outside the bounds of Beckett's career. In fact, part of what makes the novel comical is its persistent parody of the conventions of realism, as well as those of metaphysics, and the contract such a work makes with its reader. Much of the unnecessarily copious detail of the narrative is a parody of the plethora of minutiae – or 'demented particulars', as Celia's grandfather Mr Kelly dubs them (M. 12) – that underpin the verisimilitude of the realist contract. For instance, Celia is introduced at the opening of chapter 2 by a list of her 'vital statistics' run amuck to the extent that it includes the measurements of her knee, forearm and ankle to the nearest quarter-inch, prefiguring the obsessive detail with which Murphy's mind is described in chapter 6. Beckett's novel, in its anxious parody of realism, simply does not know what to leave out and, instead, overgilds the lily. While Murphy himself wants to escape the confusion of 'the big world' and choose solipsism and interiority, one could argue that Beckett as novelist is poised to make the same escape more gradually, which perhaps explains the dogged persistent presence of the 'real world' and the conventional novel through parody and pastiche.

Hugh Kenner goes so far as to suggest Murphy may be the first reader-participation novel.[6] Certainly, one at times feels the need to approach it with a good encyclopaedia or small reference library, so elaborately allusive is it. A sentence or two plucked at random may mingle Pythagorean terminology, biblical parables, Gestalt psychology and Cartesian philosophy. More importantly from the point of view of reader participation, however, is the fact that the narrative itself needs careful watching. Its self-chosen rules are close to those of the 'big world' but make frequent gestures of dissent, of varying obtrusiveness. The novel shifts in and out of the domain of verisimilitude, makes fun of causality, and casts doubt on language (the chess game conveyed via diagram). The narrator

13

frequently devotes elaborately detailed techniques to situations that are entirely impossible – despite the detail of the initial description of Murphy in his rocker, we never know how he manages to tie his own wrists to the strut behind or the location of the mysterious seventh scarf, which is left unaccounted for. It is unsettling to find that a language we all employ, devised to conform with and confirm the real world, and that in realism conventionally sets forth illusions of the familiar, lends itself to transcriptions of the impossible. Even Celia, whose emotions and motives are the stuff of standard fiction, is also a plangent lyric note unsettlingly struck against the grotesque comic vision of the rest of the novel. *Murphy* is not yet the novel of the entirely isolated self, which the trilogy would become. Not only does Murphy move in a peopled world, but narrative still provides an explicit and relatively unproblematic omniscient, if coyly self-conscious, commentary. The language of this novel has not yet quite fallen. However, signs of things to come are visible in Celia's account of Murphy's speech:

> She felt, as she felt so often with Murphy, spattered with words that went dead as soon as they sounded, each word obliterated, before it had time to make sense, by the word that came next; so that in the end she did not know what had been said. It was like difficult music heard for the first time.   (*M.* 27)

Language will more comprehensively fall in the last English fiction, *Watt*.

WATT

Begun in Paris before the German invasion, *Watt* was for the most part written in Roussillon in Vichy France, after Beckett and his partner were forced to flee from Paris in 1942 after the betrayal of their Resistance cell. The distinct note of dementia that underlies the book's surface of benign peculiarity is more easily comprehended if the reader is aware of something of the circumstances of its composition. *Watt* is the work of a writer enduring enforced stasis and physical hardship, who has seen friends arrested by the Gestapo and who has himself barely escaped capture. Beckett himself acknowledged that he wrote the novel 'to get away from war and occupation'.[7] Although it would be the last prose Beckett would write in English for many years – he had already written poetry in French, and a more decisive shift of writing languages was to come just after the war – there is already something strangely French about the English of *Watt*. The novel is full of Gallicisms – we read, for instance, about a tram's 'facultative stop' (*W*. 17) and Arsène literally enacts the slip of the tongue he is describing by beginning to say *glisser*, the French for 'to slip' (*W*. 41). We do not even need the information provided by studying the manuscript – that Beckett's marginal notes to himself start to be written in his adopted French during the composition of the novel – to realize that one of the peculiarities of *Watt* is the sense it gives of a linguistic identity buckling under intolerable pressure.[8]

Uncertainty and ambiguity haunt the narrative, although the plot is bafflingly simple. Watt, a gentle and bemused creature of strange and derelict appearance – he may not be a man at all, but 'a carpet for example, or a roll of tarpaulin' (*W*. 14) – is on a journey to take up a post as servant to a mysterious Mr Knott. After suffering various minor indignities, he arrives, displaces his predecessor, serves his term and is in his turn displaced. The book ends with Watt returning to the railway station and being abused, as he was at the outset. The narrative falls into four parts – Watt's arrival, his term as junior servant, his term as senior servant attending directly upon Mr Knott, whose rituals resemble those of the Sun King for elaborateness and formality, his departure. We also learn in the third part that Watt and the narrator, Sam, were incarcerated together in some kind of institution, and that from their encounters Sam has derived the bizarre substance of the present narrative. This explains some of the gappiness of the story, as all of Sam's information has come from Watt in dribs and drabs, and according to Watt's increasingly deranged and cryptic modes of speech, but it makes other matters still more opaque, as Sam clearly at times knows far more than Watt could have told him. Any pretensions to omniscience are thus dismantled from two sides; this narrator both knows too little and too much. And this is only one of the myriad problems of this curious narrative, in which the eternal question (Watt/what?) receives an answer that suggests both negation (Knott/not) and ensnarement (Knott/knot).

The most frequent experience of the reader of *Watt* is bafflement. Despite being encompassed with enormous, indeed frequently indigestible, amounts of factual information, none of it is 'a knowledge that could be of any help' (*W.* 36). Mr Knott, for instance, is never able to be grasped by the reader at all, despite the fact that many of his customs and habits are reported *ad nauseam* – his strange eating habits, his system of changing his position on his circular bed nightly, so as to manage a complete revolution every year. Prefiguring Godot, he remains a powerful unseen presence, defined only by negations, controlling every detail of life within his domain but espied only momentarily, brooding over his garden.

The mysteriousness of events in Mr Knott's house are implicated in the inadequacy of language to define with any certainty any object or relation. Words literally fail Watt, as his world becomes ineffable. Superficially straightforward occurrences such as the visit of the Galls to 'choon the piano' (*W.* 67) modulate into events that resist all attempts to 'saddle them with meaning' (*W.* 75). Both events and objects become recalcitrant, intractable, incapable of being mollified into meaning with words, or of themselves yielding 'semantic succour' (*W.* 79). They consent to be named, if at all, 'with reluctance', like the pot of which Watt can only say: 'It resembled a pot, it was almost a pot, but it was not a pot of which one could say, Pot, pot and be comforted' (*W.* 78). What Leslie Hill calls Watt's 'loss of filiation'[9] within language results in alienation, and a longing 'for a voice [. . .] to speak of the little world of Mr Knott's establishment, with the old words, the old credentials' (*W.* 81). The 'old credentials' of representation and unfallen language no longer have any sway in the novel.

Likewise, despite what Hugh Kenner aptly calls the novel's 'raid of syntax upon chaos', via finicky commas, scrupulous stylistic attempts to be as precise as possible, and exhaustive listings of any rational possibility, the narrative remains entwined in extreme uncertainty.[10] Watt, arriving at Mr Knott's house, is surprised to find the back door, previously locked, now open. Despite two long paragraphs enumerating the possibilities as to how the door might have been opened without Watt seeing (whether he was in fact mistaken in originally supposing it locked, or whether someone had opened it surreptitiously, and if the latter, how this was managed), the narrator concludes, straight-faced, that 'the result of this was that Watt never knew how he got into Mr Knott's house' (W. 35). Attempts at rationalization in this novel have as their result undiminished, or rather heightened, confusion. The episode of the door is also typical of the narrative movement of *Watt* as a whole, unfolding itself into a baroque edifice of possibility, before collapsing again. The most rudimentary narrative gesture cannot be made with any assurance when even the novel's most trivial events are unverifiable. Narrative movement forward becomes as problematic as Watt's extraordinary, flailing walk, his 'headlong tardigrade' (W. 28). The writing becomes so halting, riddled with commas, piling qualification upon qualification, so liable to withdraw any just-made statement, that it frequently grinds to a standstill. A. Alvarez aptly describes the prose of *Watt* as 'like a squirrel running round his treadmill: an enormous expenditure of energy of prose in order to say more or less nothing and go more or less nowhere'.[11]

While Murphy is an embattled Cartesian, Watt is a questing rationalist. Like many Beckett characters to come, he frequently lapses into arithmetic. The amused or appalled reader encounters page after page devoted to the possible combinations of notes emitted by three frogs croaking 'Krak! Krek! Krik!'; the various ways in which someone might move around a room; the family tree of the disastrous Lynches. However, while mathematics is frequently welcomed in Beckett as a comfort and stable point in a mad world, it is often exposed as faulty. It becomes apparent in *Watt* that enumerating all the permutations of the physical world will not help the puzzled enumerator to understand it. In fact, *Watt* suggests the opposite to be true; the more closely one examines the world, the more incomprehensible it becomes. *Watt* becomes, among other things, a kind of philosophical farce on rationalism; the world will not buckle down and make sense for even the most dementedly determined mind.

Watt's style bears this out. Compared to the baroque pedantry and elaborately jocular tone of *Murphy*, *Watt's* average paragraph is tirelessly explicit. It piles clause upon clause in order further to refine or explicate some odd piece of information, as though in fright that some element of, say, the (extremely funny) means by which the dog or dogs and Mr Knott's leftovers are brought together, or the permutations according to which Mrs Gorman the fishwoman and Watt sit on each other's knees, will remain unexplicated. The fact that the novel as a whole shuns the semi-colon ('How hideous is the semi-colon!' interrupts the author at one point) exacerbates the relentless march of clauses that the semi-colon might have marshalled into a more conventional relation of causal subordination. Instead, enormously long blocks of prose split helplessly among equally possible alternatives, or simultaneously accommodate more than one situation, or trail off. Yet, in the face of such rage towards the definitive and exhaustive, the events of the novel remain sunk in obscurity and incompetence, and manifest an alarming tendency to shift ground while under investigation. Madness in *Murphy* was enclosed in elegant prose, but in *Watt* style itself has flowered into full-blown psychosis.

The world of *Watt* suspends all conventional logic, while choking on its own internal amplifications and embellishments. Sections of the novel are extremely funny, and reading almost any part of the novel is amusing, but it has to be said that reading the novel in its entirety is deeply unsettling. Reading 250-odd pages of the demented obsessional reasoning by which Watt tries to apply a poultice of reason to the minor events that so disturb him, the reader becomes Watt, continually faced with situations of curiously enigmatic simplicity that evade resolution into any kind of easily available meaning. On struggling through to the end of *Watt*, there is a sting in the tail; the reader comes face to face with a set of 'Addenda', with a footnote instructing that 'The following precious and illuminating material should be carefully studied. Only fatigue and disgust prevented its incorporation' (*W.* 247). The addenda following this declaration consist of entire deleted passages, scraps of theology and poetry (one of which makes it into Beckett's *Collected Poems* at a much later date[12]), ideas for

18

episodes that never made it into the main narrative and the concluding sphinx-like admonishment that there are 'no symbols where none intended' (W. 255). In the end, the reader is not surprised that *Watt* found a publisher only in 1953, in a Paris that had responded with interest to Beckett's trilogy.

MERCIER AND CAMIER

While there would be an attractive symmetry to the notion that Beckett's obscure revelation as to the direction of his writing, just after the end of the war, immediately began to produce the indubitably mature work – the novellas, the trilogy, *Godot* – this is not in fact the case. After he changed languages, a transitional novel, in French, intervened between *Watt* and the onset of the decisively mature work of the 'siege in the room' period. *Mercier and Camier* was written in French in 1946, but Beckett did not allow it to be published until 1970, while the English translation of what he considered the last of his juvenilia did not appear until 1974. Even the tenor of his English translation, decades later, reeks of his distaste for the novel in either of its languages.[13] Although written in French, *Mercier and Camier* reads like a combination of the styles of *Murphy* and *Watt*, with the high-toned elegance of *Murphy* and the obsession with permutation and logic of *Watt*. Not surprisingly, there is virtually no plot. The eponymous heroes meet after repeatedly missing each other at the rendezvous point, procrastinate, and eventually set off on a journey, although they only briefly manage to leave town. They pass much of their time in pubs, encounter various ill-disposed authority figures, frequent an amiable whore named Helen, and kill a policeman. In between, they engage in *Godot*-like byplay with umbrellas and bicycles and engage in bar-stool metaphysics, for, as the narrator intervenes to tell us, 'it is in bars that the Merciers of this heavenly planet, and the Camiers, talk with greatest freedom, greatest profit' (*MC* 72). The insights of this conversation, typical of others throughout the novel, are summed up in numbered points, and include meditations on the absence of God, musings on the necessity for redesigning 'the male trouser', and the significance of the fact that 'soul' is

19

a four-letter word. Eventually the pair part company, but are reunited by the novel's end by Watt, apparently making a guest appearance from Beckett's previous novel.

Certainly, there is some justice in Beckett's judgement that *Mercier and Camier* is prentice-work; compared to the trilogy that followed narrowly upon its composition, it is slight indeed. However, formal innovations such as the prim, inane and misleading synopses that summarize the minimal plot every two chapters are notable for their resolute inadequacy, evoking both Beckett's increasing determination to puncture verisimilitude at every possible moment, and the increasing insignificance of plot in the mature fiction to come. The stylized absurdity of the dialogue looks ahead to *Godot*, still two years in the future, as does the fusion of descriptive passages of unexpected and muted beauty with knockabout vaudeville. In *Mercier and Camier*, Beckett has not yet – despite all efforts – managed to 'desophisticate' his writing, which is still characterized by its efforts to puncture its own knowing-ness. However, the concluding phrases of the final pseudo-summary of the novel – 'Mercier alone. Dark at its full' (*MC* 123) – already gesture ahead from this curiously retrogressive novel to the sustained mode of impotence of the novellas and trilogy.

20

2

Botched Autobiographies: The Trilogy

Beckett's trilogy of novels – *Molloy, Malone Dies* and *The Unnamable* – are by some way his most celebrated works in prose, and are some of the major prose works of the twentieth century. The trilogy was written relatively quickly, with *Molloy* begun in 1947 and *The Unnamable* completed in 1950, and the play *Waiting for Godot* embedded between *Malone Dies* and *The Unnamable*, in an intense bout of creative endeavour generally dubbed Beckett's 'siege in the room'.[1] The period of intense creativity that marks the onset of Beckett's artistic maturity emerged from what seems to have been a mid-life crisis in the immediate aftermath of the war. Able to move freely for the first time since escaping from Paris and now facing the ravages of war, he went to visit his ageing mother in Dublin, and was confronted with the fact that his most recent, still unpublished, work, *Watt*, was a stylistic dead end. In Dublin, at the age of almost 40, he underwent some form of illumination – usually identified with the seaside 'vision at last' of his 1958 play *Krapp's Last Tape*, in terms of some profound, almost ineffable, coming-to-terms with the darkness and impotence his work had tended to struggle to keep under.

Back in Paris, he wrote more copiously than ever before or after. Having, over the previous sixteen years, managed an output totalling two novels, a book of stories and one of poems, and various pieces of criticism, he would now, in less than six years, write four novellas, four novels (the trilogy and the long-suppressed *Mercier and Camier*), and two plays (*Godot* and the posthumously published *Eleuthéria*). If, as Beckett

21

stated in his piece of art criticism *Three Dialogues*, art is predicated on an impossible compromise between the recognition that there is 'nothing to express' and an equal and opposite 'obligation to express', then the trilogy manages to walk a tightrope between the two extremes, spinning a kind of discourse from endless apologies for its failure of expression, and expression performed so poorly that it arrives at a kind of apotheosis of debility.

One of the triggers for the extraordinary burst of 'impotent' creativity that found its characteristic self-cancelling voice in the trilogy was certainly Beckett's decision to write in his adopted language of French. Although after his years in France his French was fluent, and he had before the war begun to experiment with lyric poetry in French, writing prose in French represented a comprehensive break with the past. Characteristically reticent, Beckett said little in later years about this decision. He suggested obliquely and sometimes flippantly at various times that he had simply fancied a change, that writing in French was more exciting. On other occasions, perhaps more seriously, he stated that it was easier for him to write 'without style' in French, and to achieve what he dubbed 'the right weakening effect', in contrast to a native English he characterized as having 'a kind of lack of brakes'. Finally, it appears, a foreign language allowed him to escape the freighted poetry of Hiberno-English.[2]

Various critics have constructed elaborate psycho-biographical rationales for the change to French, including referencing his fear of the over-weening influence of Joyce and difficult relations with his mother as a motive for breaking with his mother tongue, but a simple comparison of the pre-war and post-war work suffices as evidence, if not explanation.[3] His pre-war style frequently runs away with him, ornate, pun-laden, seemingly at war with his austere temperament; the forms of selfhood evoked by this literary exhibitionism seem too brittle to be expressed in plain English. The style of the novellas and the trilogy, on the other hand, is both neutral and precise, sour and luminous, even as it utters the characteristically self-bankrupting sentences which the narrator of *The Unnamable* sourly refers to as 'affirmations and negations invalidated as uttered, or sooner or later' (*T.* 267). It is a style perfectly in tune with Beckett's break with the

22

traditional novel, and his shift into the plotless monologues of the trilogy.

Eric P. Levy refers to the trilogy as the 'heartland of Beckett's prose fiction', but the spatial metaphor is almost comically inappropriate.[4] Gone are the precise locations of the English fiction, to be replaced by a vague geography of unidentified town, seashore, bog, road, plain and forest, and the later, shrunken, topography of increasing claustrophobia, of bed and urn, inhabited by increasingly denatured and disembodied figures, who lose possessions, memories, limbs, even names. His move to French in fact enables this increasing move towards abstraction, allowing him to slough off the distracting mannerisms that clutter his English prose. In a new language he can arrive at a starker exploration of his perennial themes of the solitude of the isolated self, the absurdity of human existence and creative endeavour, yet the paradoxical necessity to 'stammer out your lesson', to 'go on saying words, as long as there are any' (*T*. 31).

Stripped of an English thick with associations, the influence of other voices, and a tendency to manic flourishes, the trilogy is a curiously undisguised and exposed trio of novels. It would be simplistic to suggest that it is autobiographical in any straightforward sense of the word. For one thing, it is quite the reverse of self-revelatory, though all three novels play with autobiography, and *The Unnamable*, in particular, flirts with the prurient idiom of the confessional narrative before rejecting it violently. All three, however, are peopled with solitary men writing obsessively: Molloy in his mother's room, Moran indicting his report, Malone fading between his stories in his bed, the Unnamable mysteriously managing to originate writing, despite his limblessness. In this, the trilogy flouts the convention of authorial impersonality, the dictum that the author should efface himself behind his work. In a way, it constitutes a series of novels endlessly fascinated by the circumstances of their own composition, whether by writing about the difficulties of writing and the failures of language, or the excruciatingly self-conscious disquisition on speaking and writing that forms *The Unnamable*.

While the trilogy is innovative, it does grow out of certain traditions of novel writing. Sterne's *Tristram Shandy* is continually behind Beckett's fiction, at the start of a long tradition of novels that parody the act of writing a novel, with a narrator intensely conscious of himself and of the act of writing, the empty pages to be 'blackened', as Molloy sourly puts it (*T*. 14), the compulsion to invent or 'lie', the physical motions of writing (the trilogy is full of senescent grapplings with pencil and exercise book, the preferred writing materials of Beckett's characters). The trilogy, with its cripples, tramps and journeying outcasts, certainly stands in the tradition of the picaresque novel, with its chance digressions, authorial commentaries, its marginal locale of the road. Blended with the picaresque are the existential perplexities of the incessantly self-inspecting and self-doubting narrators, which frequently take precedence over the 'story' the Beckett novel sets out to tell. The same repeated questions, variations on elements of the Western philosophical tradition, ontology and epistemology, tend to revolve in the heads of the fanatically self-narrating narrators: why exist? how can I know myself, let alone others or events? how do my body and mind relate?

The trilogy was preceded, and to some extent anticipated, by four novellas written in his adopted language in 1946, 'First Love' (only published in 1970), 'The Expelled', 'The Calmative' and 'The End' (published in conjunction with *Texts for Nothing* in 1955). The first fiction Beckett wrote in French, these four short stories are saturated with a certain muted self-surprise and unease at the new medium, and sketch a displaced exploration, via often violent images of expulsion and exile, the state of being born anew linguistically. The novellas circle about a few happenings, recounting a series of symbolic births, banishments or expulsions, which in Beckett's writing tend to be identical experiences. 'The End', for instance, opens with a derelict ejected from his abode in an asylum, his forcible clothing in unfamiliar garments that do not quite fit him, and the dismantling before his disbelieving eyes of his familiar bed. 'The Expelled' begins with the narrator's expulsion from his family home after the death of his father. The newly 'born' elderly waifs seek other forms of confinement, and uncertainly narrate texts that are virtual parables of estrangements, set in locations that are half-familiar and half-strange to the narrators, and that seem to be part Ireland, part continental

Europe: there are mentions of kepis ('The End'), the Lüneberg heath ('The Expelled'), along with typically Irish 'quiet dust-white inland roads with their hedges of hawthorn and fuchsia' (*CSP* 88). This position on a threshold also holds true in formal terms, in the sense that the mannerism of his earlier fiction is in abeyance, and there is a dawning sense, half-gratified, half-unnerved, of the novellas discovering their digressive course as they go along. The novellas are curiously liminal works, preoccupied with 'old haunts', the past and its fragments of remembered knowledge, and a nostalgia corrosively dismissed.

MOLLOY

Molloy, originally published in French in 1951, is a strange medley of a novel combining picaresque narrative, philosophical speculation, parodic humour and lyrical pathos. The narrator of its first half, Molloy, is an elderly tramp who embarks on a desultory quest for his ancient and detested mother, first on a bicycle and then on crutches, finally crawling. After various encounters and digressions – a Kafkaesque falling foul of the police for no apparent reason, being taken in for a spell by a woman possibly called Lousse as a replacement for the dog Molloy has accidentally killed, almost killing a solitary woodcutter – he ends his quest in a ditch, from which he is too enfeebled to move. From there, it is assumed, he is extricated and brought to his (presumably now dead) mother's room, where he is instructed, by a mysterious and exacting 'they', to write the story we have just read. His narrative emerges as a flow that appears to flood straight from mind to page, in which statements are made, then testily dismissed as 'rigmarole', flatly contradicted or rendered vague to the point of opacity, as though their author were consistently smudging or erasing his pencilled marks. At every faltering step, representation is endangered by the feebleness of Molloy's senses and memory, as well as by his sour distaste for the whole affair of writing, as when he announces, near the beginning of his narrative, that

> you would do better, at least no worse, to obliterate texts than to blacken margins, to fill in the holes of words till all is blank and

25

> flat and the whole ghastly business looks like what it is, senseless,
> speechless, issueless misery. (*T.* 14)

As is usual in Beckett, a plot outline conveys very little; events
are unimportant in the unparagraphed flow of Molloy's
narrative. Confusion is the norm throughout, as Molloy moves
from his few opening certainties ('I am in my mother's room')
through dawning doubt ('I don't know how I got here') to the
form of endemic uncertainty familiar from *Watt*, but here
transformed into the elegiac and yet unsettling mode that
prevails throughout the novel as a whole:

> Not to want to say, not to know what you want to say, not to be
> able to say what you think you want to say, and never to stop
> saying, or hardly ever, that is the thing to keep in mind, even in
> the heat of composition. (*T.* 27)

Molloy tells stories he does not believe in, in a language that
of its nature lies, accepting the necessity to narrate as a
mysterious punishment or penance. As he travels through an
increasingly unrecognizable and unnamable landscape, denuded even of his few remaining possessions, increasingly
weak and crippled, he enacts the pattern of diminishment that
the novel also performs at the level of style.

In *Molloy*'s second half, something akin to an opposite take
on the same story takes place. Just when it seems that further
narration by the enfeebled Molloy is impossible, a new
narrator emerges. In contrast to the destitute, crippled and
befuddled Molloy, the narrator is the comfortable bourgeois
Jacques Moran, churchgoer, authoritarian father and petty
tyrant, whose job involves mysterious activities carried out at
the behest of his immediate superior Gaber and their boss
Youdi. (The mysterious nature of the organization, and the fact
that its 'agents' are not permitted to write down their orders,
prompted early critics to see a muted allusion to Beckett's
activities in the French Resistance.) Moran's narratorial voice,
in stark contrast to Molloy's, begins in robust, meticulous
fashion, obsessively detailed and tightly paragraphed, repor-
torial. Instructed to track down Molloy (as it appears in the
past he has similarly tracked down Murphy, Watt and other
Beckett characters), he leaves his home in the company of his
son on a quest whose purpose is never asked or disclosed. The

quest for Molloy acts on Moran like a slow toxin. As Molloy gradually becomes more befuddled and decrepit over the course of his journey towards his mother's room, Moran – at the outset a minor sadist and rigid controller, devoted to domestic and religious routine – sees his ordered existence crumble, his defences fall, as he appears to become contaminated by his prey.

When he is eventually ordered by Gaber to turn back just short of Molloy's home town, he has lost his sullen son, loses the use of his legs, and, dishevelled and lame, has in fact come to resemble the man he was sent to pursue. On his return to his derelict home, with the hens and bees that symbolized his position as paterfamilias all dead, he begins to write a report, the narrative we have just read. Like Molloy, he ends a scribbling hermit, listening to wild birds and to voices in his head. As Moran prepares at the end of the narrative to set out into the world again on crutches, we are reminded of the beginning of Molloy's journey to his mother, so that the end of the novel almost adjoins the beginning. Stylistically, Moran begins by appearing to be a superior narrator, capable of narrating, capturing, defining his prey, yet he rapidly becomes as incompetent a narrator as his quarry. His initially organized narrative crumbles in its pursuit of the unattainable figment Molloy, who fragments in Moran's narrative into a multiplicity of different figures, all equally impervious to narration. In fact, Moran discredits himself entirely as both detective and narrator; he can neither find Molloy nor narrate him, just as he cannot relate the 'inenarrable contraption' that is his own life (T. 105). The novel's ending – 'I went back into the house and wrote, It is midnight. The rain is beating on the windows. It was not midnight. It was not raining' – only serves to confirm the broad hints of Moran's entire part of the novel that his narrative should not be taken at face value. The novel as a whole seems to confirm his early admission that 'it would not surprise me if I deviated, in the pages to follow, from the true and exact succession of events' (T. 122).

The parallels between Molloy and Moran often seem to hint at some large, quasi-allegorical intent on the part of the author. The resemblance of their names and Moran's vagueness as to whether his prey is not in fact called Mollose suggest the oozing arbitrariness of names in Beckett, which would culminate in the Pim, Bom, Skim, Skom and Skum of *How It Is*. Molloy wonders whether he perhaps has a son, while Moran has, at least initially, the surly and cowed Jacques Moran junior. Both narrators wax lyrical about bicycles; both lose the use of their legs and end by rolling and dragging themselves along; both violently assault a stranger who accosts them in the woods. It has frequently been suggested, for instance, that Molloy *is* Moran at a later stage of his life, and that the two halves of the novel are simply transposed from their correct chronological order. Moran's part details how a respectable bourgeois churchgoer becomes a derelict, while Molloy's chronicles this descent further, as vagrant comes completely adrift. The whole, as Hugh Kenner points out, could be read as 'one man's descent from garden and wicker chair to utter alienation'.[5]

While it is an attractive idea, since the similarities between the two narrators seem to cry out for some elucidation, to identify them with each other would be to reduce the entire novel to the level of sleight of hand, and to ignore the uncanny, almost mythic, hold that Molloy, the unseen prey, gains over his pursuer's disintegrating imagination. Eventually, Moran's quest comes to resemble Molloy's desire to find his mother, or any one of a number of literary quests, like Ahab's hunting of the whale. The mythic Molloy, who, to Moran, even before he sets off to find him, 'wears the air of a fabulous being' (*T*. 102), seems to represent a disturbing counter-image of his rational, meticulous, domesticated self and in some sense governs the process by which the bourgeois domestic tyrant is transformed, in a strange, Kafka-like metamorphosis, into the dispossessed writer-derelict.

The narrative correspondences between Molloy and Malone, in fact, while they hint at larger significance, never yield the reader enough to be going on with. Other apparent 'clues' in the novel's nomenclature also suggest but do not deliver. Gaber, we are told, is a 'messenger', and the Greek for messenger is *angelos*, suggesting (or not) that Gaber is a downmarket Angel Gabriel, complete with notebook and Sunday best. Youdi, meanwhile, is Gaber's unseen boss, suggesting the Hebrew *Yahweh* or the German *Jude* to various commentators, both God and angel converging upon Moran in a poor man's Annunciation. More centrally, Molloy's journey towards his mother has been read psychoanalytically as a primal obsession, and given deliberate Christian resonance by Molloy's references to Christ's incarnation: 'having waked between eleven o'clock and midday (I heard the angelus, recalling the incarnation, shortly after) I resolved to go and see my mother' (*T*. 16). Yet, as soon as this has been suggested, Molloy's mother, far from embodying the Virgin Mary, with child by the Holy Spirit, is evoked with Swiftian savagery as a 'deaf, blind, impotent, mad old woman', incontinent and jabbering in dentures, only a mother in the first place because her attempts at abortion misfired. The allegorical stool is kicked out from under the reader.

There is simply not the material to construct any kind of adequate allegory. Like the hints of detective-story format, Beckett's name-games and perennial suggestiveness are simply another of his devices for giving his narratives a sense of near-intelligibility. He hints at a pattern that will not really fit, or at least certainly not in the way that the episodes of Joyce's *Ulysses* correspond to the *Odyssey*. If, as Andrew Kennedy suggests, *Molloy* represents a kind of anti-*Pilgrim's Progress*, a *Pilgrim's Regress*, it is to no obvious divine goal and with fading resources and purpose.[6] What the half-familiarity of aspects of *Molloy* does is to settle the reader in a world that seems to be about to cohere, but then dissolves. In this, it performs similarly to individual paragraphs or even sentences, which dwindle into increasing inconsequence and confusion, while retaining their curious precision in sculpting the void. As with Molloy's anxious permutation of his pebbles in the celebrated sucking stones episode, Moran's narrative reshuffles the elements of Molloy's; the art of the novel, if it no longer expresses anything, retains a certain pleasure in the recombination of abstract essentials.

MALONE DIES

Malone Dies, the second trilogy novel, was written as *Malone meurt* in 1947–8 and published in French in 1951. It represents a further spiral towards depletion, having only one voice, less plot and, as sole narrator, a sour octogenarian on his deathbed whose only ambition is to finish his long-drawn-out dying, a grotesque 'old foetus [. . .] hoar and impotent', waiting to 'land head-foremost and mewling in the charnel-house' (*T*. 207). As the title implies, this unpromising aspiration provides the sole continuity of the novel. Residual traces of plot keep dissolving into nothing, and everything gets left in the air, even Malone's death, 'when it will be all over with the Murphys, Merciers, Molloys, Morans and Malones, unless it goes on beyond the grave' (*T*. 217). This is Beckett's first usage of death as an infinitely postponed or inconclusive conclusion, which will also structure later works such as *Endgame*. *Malone Dies* is at least as much of a generic ragbag as *Molloy*, with the dregs of a 'story' flowering out into Cartesian musings, meditations on ageing and death, the nature of suffering, the anonymity and debasement of urban life, original sin and, above all, the mysterious 'I', the self that remains inexplicably fastened to the dying animal of the body. While the quest-motif structured *Molloy*, the deathbed memoir, though savagely parodied, offers a residual pattern to *Malone Dies*, which retains comic elements of some Victorian paterfamilias grandly disposing of his possessions. These elements, however, are dwindled and parodied by Beckett's pen into Malone's account of his minimal 'chattels personal' – one boot, the bowl of a pipe and a newspaper-wrapped package.

Malone seems to exist in the backwash of Molloy's and Moran's narratives; his ancestry is certainly rooted in the closed world of Beckett's previous novels, which *Malone Dies*, with its panoply of references to previous Beckett characters, effectively subsumes. Bedridden, confined to a room whose location and function he does not know, Malone retains among his few possessions a bicycle bell and a crutch which imply a link to the characters in the preceding novel. (He also makes reference to a bloodstained club, memories of a forest and a blow on the head, so it is possible that he is one of the men the narrators of *Molloy* attacked. Beckett, however, goes no further with these clues, which seem to be residual, half-amused, half-contemptuous gestures towards a kind of continuity in which he is no longer interested.) Like Molloy, he has no recollection of his arrival at this, his final destination. Like both Molloy and Moran, he is compelled to write, with a dwindling stub of pencil in a child's copybook, although the resources on which he can draw for his fiction are neither so explicitly autobiographical nor so copious as theirs. He decides that he will pass the time till his imminent death by compiling an inventory of his possessions, and in telling four stories 'almost lifeless, like the teller'. One of these will be 'about a man, one about a woman, one about a thing and finally one about an animal, a bird probably' (*T*. 166). His death and the end of his narrative will, of necessity, coincide.

However, Malone manages only the first of these projected stories, about a brooding, alienated boy called Sapo or Saposcat (possibly a combination of 'homo sapiens' and 'scatological') who rejects his penny-pinching bourgeois parents and grows into a typical Beckett vagrant (Macmann, or 'son of man'), and who strikingly resembles Malone himself. Macmann, his name emphasizing his kinship with Beckett's other M-heroes, having wandered through the anonymous wasteland of urban life, ends his days confined to an asylum, the House of St John of God. There he is nursed and consoled by an equally ancient woman, Moll, who is chiefly remarkable for having her one remaining tooth carved into the likeness of a crucifix. Their ghastly amours are recounted with a combination of Swiftian enjoyment of the grotesque, a bravura skit on the conventions of romantic love, and a halting tenderness.

Macmann's story ends abruptly with most of the characters arbitrarily killed off by a hatchet-wielding maniac called Lemuel, apparently because their dying author is abruptly tired of them. Lemuel, Macmann and the surviving inmates drift out to sea in a boat, as Malone's pencil appears to record the 'gurgles of outflow' of his final drift towards death:

> Lemuel is in charge, he raises his hatchet on which the blood will never dry, but not to hit anyone, he will not hit anyone, he will not hit anyone any more, he will not touch anyone any more, either with it or with it or with it or with or
> or with it or with his hammer or with his stick or with his fist or in thought or in dream I mean never he will never
> or with his pencil or with his stick or
> or light light I mean

31

never there he will never
never anything
there
any more   (T. 264)

In this final eerie, staccato passage, Lemuel's impotently flailing hatchet stands proxy for Malone's lost stick, dwindling pencil and failing life. It has been clear from the very start of the Sapo/Macmann 'story' that it is no simple time-passing entertainment but has a metaphysical purpose. The life of Malone's 'hero' becomes quickly imbued with his own personal memories, which stubbornly and often despairingly erupt into the otherwise placid narrative surface. As one critic has noted, the relation between Malone and his creature is notable for a 'certain horrified intimacy';[7] attempting to breathe life into the heterogeneous collection of human scraps that constitute his creature, Malone hopes to implicate his unnarratable self with Macmann, and, in killing the latter, also release himself into silence, from the appalling obligation to continue to tinker with stories and attempts to 'eff' the 'ineffable' self. It is in sabotaging his mock persona, ramshackle and unconvincing as Sapo/Macmann is, that Malone comes closest to a kind of self-expression, or botched autobiography.

Malone Dies was always conceived of as a companion novel to *Molloy* and shares its imperfect and crabwise dualism in less obvious ways. Where *Molloy* was riven between the narratives of Molloy and Moran, the second trilogy novel alternates between present immobility and senescence (passages in which Malone describes the loss of his stick and pencil, or a mysterious seven-hour visit from a silent stranger, possibly an early undertaker, the fact that his food and chamber pot are no longer brought by an anonymous 'withered hand') and the story with which Malone is amusing himself. Starting out as entirely separate, story and life coalesce gradually, as the story character ends up as old and confined as his creator. Malone's story is itself also double. The dull-witted child Sapo, first evoked in the company of his colourless parents, then with the brutish Lamberts, appears to change his name en route to becoming the elderly vagrant Macmann, as if by analogy with Molloy and Moran. We do not see his growing up, or receive

32

any explanation for the change of nomenclature, far less any guarantee that the two are in fact one character. Sapo/ Macmann appears to have a certain autonomy from the man who is making him up (and using him as a foil or mask for a displaced autobiography), and Malone only 'finds' him again as an old man, altered by 'life perhaps, the struggle to love, to eat, to escape the redressers of wrongs' (*T.* 208).

Whether or not they are semi-autonomous characters, it is quickly evident that there is no stable distance between Sapo/ Macmann and Malone. His self is not ideally timeless, and he has receded so far from the world that all usual means of self-definition has broken down, so that his 'I' is no more recognizable at the end of his life than at the beginning. In his stories Malone seeks to abandon the persona 'Malone' and 'on the threshold of being no more [. . .] succeed in being another' (*T.* 178). Stories, he hopes, may help him to reach himself, so that, in killing his fictional character and other self, he can release himself into death via a kind of sympathetic magic. However, the Beckettian vicious circle – writing in order to absolve yourself from the obligation of writing, speaking in order to be eventually allowed to be silent – is more vicious in *Malone Dies* than in *Molloy*. Malone realizes from the outset that he 'shall not succeed any better than hitherto' and will only end up finding himself 'abandoned in the dark, without anything to play with' (*T.* 166).

The Cartesian dualism familiar from *Murphy* and *Molloy* is also a continual preoccupation. Malone, in this novel, which has, as he says, 'fled into the head' – at one point he hints that 'these six planes that surround me are of solid bone' (*T.* 203) – continues to meditate on the mysterious involvement of body and mind, but in a less frenzied manner than his predecessors. He accepts the limitations of his progressive decline, and that his terrain is now the bed in which he sits, naked, hairy, toothless and impotent. He is reliant (like Molloy on his bicycle and crutches) on the stick or proxy body by which he satisfies his needs, rooting among his possessions, and hooking soup and chamber pot within reach. If from time to time he forgets his decay and gives his shrivelled old body 'the old orders I know it cannot obey', he is in general resigned to the fact that his body is so ineffectual and so remote that it might well be at an infinite distance from his mind. In true Cartesian form, he spatializes this by insisting on a kind of exaggerated geography of distance that divides mind and ailing body. His feet are 'leagues away' from his head – 'for that is where I am fled' (T. 215) – and when his stick slips from his grasp, he says it might as well be as far from him as the equator; he is left marooned in his own Cartesian geography. Now that his body has entirely deserted him, he can pass the boredom of his last hours only by peopling his crumbling silence with the 'creatures' of his stories.

It is also the final decay of the body that strands Malone, and the Beckett narrators to come, in a universe of pure language, disturbingly aware that he is himself no more than a persona in another narrator's play of words, aware of 'a blind and tired hand delving feebly in my particles' (T. 215). He is helpless before the flux of language – 'words and images run riot in my head, pursuing, flying, clashing, merging endlessly' (T. 182) – that the novel foregrounds, dissolving the illusion of any adequate representational correspondence between narrating subject and narrated object. *Malone Dies* manages to achieve in its closing passages a kind of eerie serenity, what Malone dubs 'the immutable relations between harmoniously perishing items' (T. 210). Part of this is certainly a nihilistic satisfaction, the result of Beckett's satisfaction in having taken a hatchet to the traditional novel, and cleared the way for his later experiments in the meta- or post-novel. In the succeeding novels and plays Beckett returns very rarely to the world of the living from which Malone takes leave. From now on in Beckett's writing, there is only silence and voice or voices, continuing to talk.

THE UNNAMABLE

If, at the end of *Malone Dies*, the self has dissolved, in *The Unnamable*, the trilogy's concluding volume (written in French in 1949–50, published 1953), that self is revived, or has at least not been conclusively ended by death. It is as though Beckett's corrosive pessimism will not allow him to believe that the death of Malone would provide any kind of resolution or end to the problem of speaking the ineffable self in language. The voices, it seems, and the compulsion to narrate, to go on in words, continue beyond the grave into the limbo or purgatory that succeeds it, and in which the Unnamable is confined. However, the traditional *content* of the novel – the characters and plots that make fiction satisfying – has not survived the purge of *Malone Dies*, and only the metaphysical problem of writing, barely, if lengthily, stated, remains in this shapeless monster of an anti-novel. This time the reader is not in the presence of a Molloy, Moran or Malone. Indeed, the voice of *The Unnamable* cannot truly be termed a narrator, or character, although it is driven to narrate as compulsively as its predecessors, because this creature exists only as a side effect of words; it is there only as long as it speaks. While Molloy and Malone begin in their different rooms, the Unnamable begins only within the confines of language:

> Where now? Who now? When now? Unquestioning. I, say I. Unbelieving, Questions, hypotheses, call them that. Keep going, going on, call that going, call that on [. . .] (*T.* 267)

All the appurtenances of fiction have been abandoned, and the novel is without beginning or end apart from the arbitrary start and finish given it by print and paper. Punctuation is soon cast aside, apart from a staccato of breathless commas, and the text plunges forward under the impetus of an anarchy of words, becoming ever more frenzied and unrestrained.

What emerges from this torrent of language is a succession of fragments – brief flashes of meaning, short passages of description, introductions and sometimes instantaneous repudiations of characters, lightning changes of direction – all poured forth in an unstoppable flood, like an existential parody of Molly Bloom's monologue. *The Unnamable*, in fact, is a monologue that becomes, after the first dozen or so pages, a single, seemingly endless, paragraph. It is spoken from some fathomless post-mortem space, by a kind of proto-creature, who describes himself variously as 'like a great horn-owl in an aviary' (*T.* 269), 'a big talking ball' (*T.* 280), 'liquefied brain' (*T.* 269) and a grotesquely imprisoned live advertisement for a backstreet chop-house, grinding his unstoppable 'wordy-gurdy' (*T.* 301). Although he claims part of the time that he is limbless and naked, at others, he wears shreds of rags and puttees. Immobile and confined, he does not know how he is able to write, 'to consider only the manual aspect of that bitter folly', but stares fixedly ahead with eyes that 'must be as red as live coals' (*T.* 276). The underworld he inhabits is dark and featureless, apart from scant gleams of light that show him the forms of previous Beckett characters, such as Mercier and Camier and Malone – whom he repudiates as 'vice-existers' or 'delegates', whose construction occluded his attempts to speak his self in language – revolving about him like satellites about a sun. While he retains some unreliable memories, like all Beckett's men, of his mother, a Calvinistically inclined religious doctrine, and his detested 'unfamiliar native land', his is the essentially posthumous existence for which Beckett's protagonists have often pined, 'a little hell after my own heart, not too cruel, with a few nice damned to foist my groans on' (*T.* 280).

However, in the bleaker vision of *The Unnamable*, posthumous life, for those guilty of the original sin of having been born, offers no solace to the torment of the speaker, his compulsion to go on talking. At one point he compares himself to Prometheus, punished by the gods, but the vulture tearing at the Unnamable's innards is language, the 'strange task, which consists in speaking of oneself'. He is condemned to the 'churn of words', and the necessity of endlessly speaking them, as Sisyphus to his rock, or any of Dante's damned to their persecutions:

> I have to speak, whatever that means. Having nothing to say, no words but the words of others, I have to speak. No one compels me, there is no one, it's an accident, a fact [. . .] I have the ocean to drink [. . .]   (*T.* 288)

The Unnamable's punishment – to speak endlessly of himself – is also Beckett's novelist's obsession; each writes, or speaks, until he hits upon the matter that must be spoken or written in order to be absolved from the need to write or speak, on the model of the sinner suffering after death to redeem his sins on earth. The salvation to be worked or spoken or suffered towards is longed-for silence: 'my speech-parched voice at rest would fill with spittle, I'd let it flow over and over, happy at last, dribbling with life, my pensum ended, in the silence [. . .]' (*T*. 284).

As with the other trilogy novels, and other Beckett works in which a figure is interrogated or goaded into unwilling speech, earlier critics read a Gestapo theme: the tormented man required to talk, but who fears he does not in fact possess the information his torturers must be made to think they have extracted. All he has said before – the previous fictions of Samuel Beckett, almost all referred to by name – is inauthentic and must be set aside as so much wasted breath and blackened paper: 'All these Murphys, Molloys and Malones do not fool me. They have made me waste my time, suffer for nothing, speak of them, when, in order to stop speaking, I should have spoken of me and me alone' (*T*. 278).

These 'vice-existers' have purported to represent the Unnamable, 'up there in the world', in fraudulent fashion, 'walling me about with their vociferations'. There is a horror and a pathos also in the narrative's wincing decision to eschew these 'delegates' for 'the obligation, once rid of them, to begin again, to start again from nowhere, from no one and from nothing' (*T*. 277) and 'say of me that I see this, feel that, fear, hope, know and do not know?' (*T*. 273).

As is usual for a Beckett narrator, the Unnamable tries telling stories, though far more sporadically and with still less conviction than in the previous two novels. The novel proceeds in its headlong manner by repudiation; every effort the Unnamable makes to free himself from fictions generates more fictions, which, as the novel goes on, are posited and dismantled at increasing speed. To escape from the frame story, in which previous Beckett characters orbit the speaker, the Unnamable turns his attention to a grotesque story about the one-legged Mahood, circling excruciatingly slowly back from a world tour to his numerous next of kin, only to find, by the time he reaches them, they have all died of food poisoning. Another long episode concerns Mahood (now increasingly inextricable from the sketchy and alarmingly itinerant 'I' of the narrator), now legless and armless, stuck in a jar across from a restaurant, acting as advertisement and freakish menu-holder for its proprietress. When Mahood threatens to become too engaging and vivid, he is abandoned for the more muted subsidiary 'character' Worm. When Worm in turn appears too substantially human and fully present, he is forsaken in his turn for a long, flickering succession of unnamed momentary figments, abandoned as rapidly as conceived. The indeterminacy of the 'I', already pronounced in the trilogy's two previous novels, reaches its apotheosis; the Unnamable can do nothing to resist any name foisted on him, despite all his attempts at repudiation. Unnamable, he is both essentially shapeless and a confusing multitude of shapes, as he is constructed and dismantled, murdered and created, by this stream of near-gibberish.

The Unnamable is a work of scalding linguistic scepticism, certainly partly because it is the single work in which Beckett most nakedly confronts the foreignness of the language in which he has chosen to write, which speaks him, rather than is spoken by him. It is also significant that the trilogy as a whole was underwritten by hundreds of thousands of words of jobbing translation, and that he was translating passages of *Molloy* into English as he worked on *The Unnamable*. It is a manifestly translatorial novel, concerned with a voice hoarse from voicing the speech of others, which has said 'I' so often for the purposes of another's narrative, for which it acts as loudspeaker or ventriloquist's dummy, that it cannot see the possibility of wringing anything from language but further impasses of grammatical insincerity.[8] Words in *The Unnamable* traverse the self, they do not guarantee or express it: 'the words swarm and jostle like ants, hasty and indifferent, bringing nothing, taking nothing away, too light to leave a mark' (*T*. 326). Selfhood is nothing more than either passive submission to one's construction by words that are the property of another and that cannot be wrenched around to one's own purposes, or futile wranglings with a prior and foreign discourse, to which one is unalterably subject. The literary text is impersonal, writing itself, with the author as mere amanuensis.

Beckett's project in the trilogy, then, is twofold: to debunk the traditional structure of the novel as linear quest in which a subject progresses through development to discovery, often the discovery of a real or transcendent self, and, secondly, to dismantle the idea of the omniscient narrator as a mode of privileged discourse. Beckett, in parodying Molloy, Moran, Malone and the Unnamable as authors, sabotages the claim of 'classical realism' to meaning; words in the trilogy never correspond to reality, and Molloy admits at one point that 'what really happened was quite different'. The narrating ego is thus doomed from the start, and we have instead a progressive decline into narrative anarchy.

3

Fearful Symmetries: *Waiting for Godot* to *Play*

Samuel Beckett wrote the two plays for which he is best known, *Waiting for Godot* and *Endgame*, in the middle phase of his writing career. *Waiting for Godot* was originally written in French, as *En attendant Godot*, between October 1948 and January 1949, in the midst of a frenetic burst of writing often dubbed the 'siege in the room'. *Endgame* was also first written in French, as *Fin de partie*, in 1955–6, after *The Unnamable* had signalled the end of Beckett's frenzy of prose. Interrelations between the prose and drama are complex, as though the impulse into drama that spurred the writing of *Godot* was a way of both escaping from and controlling the weight of barely speakable anguish and linguistic alienation of the trilogy – and perhaps the great prose torrents of *The Unnamable* were made possible by the strict control of stage space in *Godot*. The impact produced by these plays, both on Beckett's own career, and on post-war European drama, was prodigious. For instance, the *succès de scandale* of the first productions, in French and English, of *Godot* speedily transported him from almost complete obscurity to fame, not to say notoriety. Furthermore, in its utter disregard of existing theatrical convention, *Godot* catapulted the theatrical world into excitement and perplexity. By the time *Endgame* was first staged in London in 1958, Beckett's emergence as a dramatist of exceptional originality and radicalism was confirmed. The briefer plays of the later 1950s and 1960s, with their pronounced formal innovation playing against a patently diminished concept of theatre, served only to cement his reputation. Critics hailed his starkly

40

vivid stage images as the achievement of a previously inarticulable post-war experience, and as heralding the emergence of a new kind of drama.

WAITING FOR GODOT

Waiting for Godot has long been established as one of the defining works of twentieth-century European culture. It is a particular touchstone in an art form that was throughout much of the twentieth century a particular chronicler of failure and defeat. Even though it is often difficult to be very specific about the ways in which *Godot* is 'about' war, it was written shortly after the end of a world war that had shaken traditional beliefs and provoked massive migrations of people, leaving millions uprooted and starving. Horror at the cruelties of life, as well as anguish at its uncertainties, are feelings never far from the surface of *Godot*. At the same time, the themes around which the play circles – waiting, uncertainty and the problem of human existence in time; the symbiotic relationship of the couple; the contrast between human aspiration and reality; the tension between comedy and tragedy in everyday situations – are mundane to the point of banality. It is this tension between the mundane and the existential, the concrete and the metaphysical, vaudeville slapstick and pervasive melancholy that makes its various levels of meaning difficult to exhaust.

The boldness with which *Godot* undermined dramatic convention caused considerable sensation, and the play immediately compelled a large amount of critical attention. One of the characteristic tones of the earliest responses and reviews – both positive and negative – is puzzlement, and a wariness about the applicability of critical terminology. Jacques Lemarchand, reviewing the first-ever performance of the French *Godot*, in the tiny Parisian Théâtre de Babylone, comments that '*Waiting for Godot* is a profoundly original work: because of this it will necessarily be a disconcerting one.'[1] Likewise, in his review of the first English performance of *Godot*, at the London Arts Theatre Club in 1955, Kenneth Tynan observes: '*Waiting for Godot* frankly jettisons everything by which we recognise theatre [. . .] It forced me to re-examine the rules which have

41

hitherto governed the drama; and, having done so, to pronounce them not elastic enough.'[2] However, it is not simply that *Godot* refused to conform to recognizable dramatic convention, but, more alarmingly, that it threatened to discard convention altogether. *Godot* so thoroughly abandons the notion of the well-made play that it frequently appears to be about to cease being a play, or actively to attack the idea of a play. One critic would later describe *Godot* as an 'anti-play' and as a 'parody of the dramatic'.[3]

Certainly, *Godot*, famously the 'play in which nothing happens, twice',[4] is ill served by the conventional critical approach of summarizing the plot and characters. Even to give a summary of the 'action' is awkward, as the play purposely sets out to explode traditional notions of theatrical construction, whereby meaning can be extracted through exposition, crisis and denouement. If we persist in looking at *Godot* from the perspective of plot – as a coherent series of events, following in some kind of sequential order, and explaining each other – then the source of the frustration quickly becomes evident. The play consists of two acts, the second repeating the broad outline of the first, with minor variations. Two friends, Vladimir and Estragon, known to each other as Didi and Gogo, wait uneasily by a tree on a country road for a mysterious figure named Godot, whom they expect to save them. While waiting, they engage in formulaic backchat, sing songs, and perform old-style comic routines with shoes, vegetables and bowler hats. They briefly encounter a master, Pozzo, and his burdened servant, the ironically-named Lucky, who linger a while with them, and then depart again. A young boy arrives with a message purporting to be from the elusive Godot, saying that he will not come that evening, but will certainly come the next. Night falls and the moon rises, and the two men decide to go, but do not move. In a different and more traditional type of play, these events would be elucidated and the questions continually raised – are the men even in the right place? who is Godot? will he save them? – would be resolved, but in Beckett's hands answers to these questions are perpetually deferred. The audience remains as anxious and uncertain as Vladimir and Estragon.

The opening words of the play establish its theme:

42

ESTRAGON. Nothing to be done.
VLADIMIR. I'm beginning to come round to that opinion.

(*CDW* 11)

While Estragon is in fact referring to his ill-fitting boots, and when Vladimir repeats the phrase later in the play it refers to his hat, they are talking about their lives, habit and boredom, and the necessity of finding ways to pass the time. Essentially, *Godot* dramatizes themes Beckett first voiced in his monograph on Proust, and went on to explore throughout the intervening prose: 'Habit is a compromise effected between the individual and his environment, or between the individual and his own organic eccentricities, the guarantee of dull inviolability, the lightning conductor of his existence' (*PTD* 18–19).

Vladimir in *Godot*, near the end of the play, and with its entire weight of boredom and despair behind him, says the same thing more simply: 'Habit is a great deadener' (*CDW* 84). What we see during the play is the tramps attempting to fend off the emptiness and silence, the 'suffering of being' Beckett discusses in his *Proust* – making itself felt in jabs of physical pain, and moments of existential anguish – with ritualized byplay and banter. Anything that passes time is eagerly grasped at. The long silence following Lucky and Pozzo's first visit is broken by Vladimir saying 'That passed the time.' When Estragon sourly says that 'it would have passed in any case', Vladimir retorts, 'Yes, but not so rapidly.' Generally, both tramps conspire in the desperately amusing game to keep suffering at bay: 'That's the idea, let's make a little conversation' (*CDW* 46). But, like the disconcertingly long pauses that perforate the play, such inventiveness always runs out. Nothingness is always pushing through the brittle shell of slapstick and chaff.

Just as *Godot*'s characters manœuvre through empty stage space to pass the time during their wait, so too does the audience forcibly participate in the experience. Beckett originally thought of calling his play *En attendant* [*Waiting*] in order to deflect the attention of readers and spectators away from the mysterious Godot onto the act of waiting. Similarly, he also firmly deleted the *Wir* [we] from the original title of the German translation of *Waiting for Godot*, *Wir warten auf Godot*

43

[*We're waiting for Godot*], so that audiences would not focus too much upon the individuality of the characters, but would be forced instead to think about all existence as a waiting. In the play, the act of waiting – both onstage and in the audience – operates as a complex metaphor for human existence. Martin Esslin points out in the introduction to his influential *The Theatre of the Absurd* that, in staging the act of waiting and in forcing the audience to undergo the same experience in real time, Beckett is 'trying to capture the basic experience of being "in the world", having been thrust into it without a by-your-leave, and having, somehow, to come to terms with "being there" *Dasein* itself, in Heidegger's sense'.[5]

Vladimir and Estragon are therefore hardly 'characters' at all in the traditional sense – readers, rather than spectators, of the play have always found them virtually impossible to distin-guish from each other – and have no role other than literally to 'be there'. Unsure of their own identities, with no memories or facts on which they can agree, uncertain as to why they need Godot, or whether they are in the right place, they endure time, degenerate slightly but tellingly throughout the two acts, and, above all, lapse into self-conscious physical and verbal routines just to fill the silence and ward off their fear of the void. As Estragon says: 'We always find something, eh Didi, to give us the impression that we exist?' (*CDW* 64).

As an alternative to the well-made play, *Godot* leaves us with nothing but what Geneviève Serreau has termed 'pure play'.[6] As well as the absence of plot *Godot* borrows from vaudeville or circus, character becomes nothing more than a set of comic oppositions, as the point of a pair of comedians' act may be nothing more than physical or temperamental incompatibility. One clown may be happy, one sad, one tall, one short, and from this may spring the root of a series of routines. Character in *Godot* partakes of some of this kind of rudimentariness, and, while some critics have attempted to 'round out' Vladimir and Estragon into more fully conceived characters, this is rarely convincing, and is certainly not what the *Godot* audience experiences. Rather than attempting to fill out these scraps into convincing 'rounded' characters, then, it makes considerably more sense to approach each of the pair – Didi and Gogo, Pozzo and Lucky – as two halves of a single theatrical dynamic. Pozzo and Lucky are very obviously interlinked by the classic interdependence of master and slave. They are even literally fastened together by the rope fastened around the burdened and weak Lucky's neck, which the well-fed and autocratic Pozzo holds like a dog leash. However, even though Pozzo appears to be in command throughout, even commanding Lucky to dance and 'think' aloud as entertainment, there are suggestions that Pozzo is dependent on Lucky also, a situation to be explored in *Endgame*.

With no such obvious imbalance of power, Vladimir and Estragon are linked by a series of far more minor comic contrasts – Vladimir has stinking breath, while Estragon has stinking feet; Estragon's feet hurt him, while Vladimir's prostate is his main physical problem. Vladimir wants to hear Lucky think, Estragon to see him dance. Vladimir tends towards agitation, Estragon towards boredom and inertia. Many critics have elaborated on this importance of shape in *Godot*, pointing out the presence of symmetries and oppositions within the twinned acts and twinned couples. Specifically linguistic shaping is also important; for instance, the song that opens Act II is not significant because of any inherent meaning, but because it is structured like a potentially endless cycle, like the play itself, while at the other extreme of the play's stylized language is Lucky's speech, constructed of disjointed fragments of theological argument, conveying the shape of a mind breaking down, like Watt's, when confronted with an illogical world.

Many early theatre-goers perceived the play as essentially symbolic. Stripped to its crude outline, Beckett's play certainly does sound like an allegory or fable, which has most often been read in Christian terms, with the mysterious Godot as a Messiah the tramps expect to bring them salvation, but whose continually postponed appearance keeps them hanging onto life, tethered to the same spot, endlessly hoping their suffering and boredom will be redeemed. From this central identification of Godot as a kind of *Deus Absconditus* (the suggestion of the name strengthened for early commentators by mentions of his white beard and punitive tendencies, as well as 'prayer' and 'supplication'), other allegorical readings were elaborated. (According to such readings, Pozzo and Lucky, for instance, are, variously, Body and Intellect, Master and Slave, Capitalist

45

and Proletarian, Colonizer and Colonized, Cain and Abel, Sadist and Masochist, even Joyce and Beckett.[7])

However, Beckett said in later years that 'the early success of *Waiting for Godot* was based on a fundamental misunderstanding; critics and public alike insisted on interpreting in allegorical and symbolical terms a play which was striving all the time to avoid definition'.[8] Whenever directors or critics asked for explanations of Godot, he both sidestepped their questions and revealed his distrust of any kind of exegesis; to Alan Schneider's question 'Who or what does Godot mean?', he replied, 'If I knew, I would have said so in the play.'[9] More recent commentaries have tended to be less dogmatic in their readings of the play. A. Alvarez argues that the mysterious Godot (the suffix '-ot' in French implying a diminutive often used in nicknames) is what his name implies: 'just another diminutive god like all the other little gods – some divine, some political, some intellectual, some personal – for whom men wait, hopefully and in fear, to solve their problems and bring point to their pointless lives.'[10] Godot is primarily an absence, who can be interpreted at moments as God, or death, but Godot has a *function* rather than a *meaning*.[11] He stands for what keeps us chained to and in existence, he is the unknowable that represents hope in a hopeless era, he is whatever fiction or figment we want him to be – as long as he justifies lives spent in waiting.

Failed or foiled rationalism, leading only to uncertainty, disappointment and oddly inconclusive conclusions reminiscent of *Watt*, are certainly an important element in the play's effect. Beckett himself, famously unwilling or unable to elucidate his plays for actors or directors, commented that the keyword in his theatre is 'perhaps',[12] and the notebooks he prepared for his own production of *Godot* direct attention to the radical uncertainty that characterizes the entire play. In an interview with Israel Shenker, Beckett makes an explicit opposition between the writings of his revered James Joyce and his own, saying 'the more Joyce knew, the more he could'; Beckett himself, in contrast, is a 'non-knower, a non can-er'.[13] Vladimir and Estragon are certainly this, and the whole play partakes of this incapacity and uncertainty. The essential qualities of uncertainty, ignorance and impotence that define the lives of the characters emerge in the form of hundreds of questions that receive no answers, stories that are never concluded, actions left deliberately unexplained, and, perhaps most powerfully, in the form of concrete, visual images that reveal man as essentially befuddled, disoriented and bewildered.

ENDGAME

If *Godot* is based on the premiss of an arrival that never occurs, then *Endgame* is premissed on a departure that never happens, and an ending that is always close at hand but never entirely here. The play was first staged in French at London's Royal Court Theatre in 1957. Like *Godot*, it combines extreme, even unnerving, dramatic simplicity with the potential for being read symbolically. Vivian Mercier, for instance, reads it as 'a play about the end of the world'.[14] Harold Clurman, in a review of the Manhattan Theatre Club's 1980 production, as 'a Mystery of final things: death, the end of an age'.[15] Beckett's own favourite play, *Endgame*, makes use of elements he has employed before: the game of chess, the ambivalent master–servant relationship, the man in a chair, the telling of a story equivocally related to the life of the teller, casually ritualized cruelty, speech eerily eroded by silences. *Endgame* is played out, claustrophobically, in a single room, like the rooms to which Molloy and Malone are brought after their wanderings end. Of its four characters, only Clov, the sullen slave, can move about, albeit with the usual Beckett 'stiff, staggering walk' (*CDW* 92). Hamm, his master, is blind and crippled, helpless yet domineering, confined to a wheelchair, while Hamm's parents, his 'accursed progenitor[s]' (*CDW* 96), the absurdly courtly Nell and Nagg, are superannuated amputees kept, surreally, in dustbins, as though to concretize their geriatric expendability. Theirs is a world marked by increasing deprivation; there are, for instance, no longer any bicycle wheels, or pap for the toothless gums of the ancient parents, and at one point Clov remarks 'there's no more nature', at least 'in the vicinity' (*CDW* 97).

The opening of the play sees the small windows high up on the rear wall curtained, and Hamm and the bins draped with

47

dustsheets, like disused furniture. Clov's first task is to draw the curtains, give a contemptuous look outside, and remove the sheets, in a patent metaphor for waking up, on a set that resembles the interior of a skull with two eyeholes. Beckett's drama has moved away from the relative naturalism of the *Godot* set, and has retreated into an eerie inner space, which also, contrarily, through references to the room as 'the shelter', outside of which is a 'corpsed' landscape and 'death', suggests a post-nuclear world. (This 'endgame' would then be the last hours of the final vestiges of human life.) In contrast to the traditional symbolism of the road – suggesting progress, quest, movement – which is parodied in *Godot*, *Endgame* draws on the equally established trope of room-as-mind. However, this nightmarish room, with its confined, tormented inhabitants, is in stark contrast to the attractive solipsism conjured up by the padded cell in *Murphy*.

Endgame gets by on even less plot than *Godot*. Recounting infinitesimally small non-events on a run-of-the-mill day, the play, as Beckett said in a letter to the director Alan Schneider, depends 'on the power of the text to claw' (*D.* 107). What we see on stage, in this wretched room, is a mere series of (mostly verbal) entertainments concocted to pass Hamm's dreary day. In this, it resembles *Godot*, but with the horrifying difference that in *Endgame* there is nothing to wait for, except another tranquillizer or biscuit, another circuit around the small available space. Over the course of the play's single act, Hamm emerges as a petty bully with delusions of grandeur hardened into a monstrous egotism, with authorial ambitions, and a chillingly loveless relationship with his parents, whom he hates for conceiving him. He seems to suffer from a kind of hereditary lovelessness, cursing his father for engendering him, being cursed in return, with Nagg's current wretched condition mirroring his neglect of the child Hamm: 'We let you cry. Then we moved you out of earshot, so that we might sleep in peace' (*CDW* 119). Clov, body to Hamm's mind, is deformed by servitude, and, despite the fact that he claims he would kill Hamm if he himself knew the combination of the larder, seems bound to him by a kind of contemptuous compassion. The pathetic parents reminisce and make childlike demands from their bins. The play's only event occurs towards the end, when

Clov spies from the window a boy sitting in the distance in the desolate landscape, and Hamm fears the human race will be regenerated from him, as he deems complete extinction desirable. He declares all is over and dismisses Clov in apparent anticipation of his own death, but, though Clov reappears clad in travelling clothes, he never finally leaves the stage, although the blind Hamm assumes he has gone.

Endgame abounds in hints and haunting quasi-allusions: the actorly blind storyteller Hamm variously suggests Shakespeare's Hamlet, Lear and Prospero, or, it has been suggested, James Joyce, in his fidelity to his stories through pain and tribulation. Per Nykrog reads him as a 'hideous caricature of the hypertrophied, nineteenth-century Ego in its death throes'.[16] Hugh Kenner suggests Hamm may be a reduced post-Nietzschean dying god, blind and tyrannical, attended by Clov as demiurge, withdrawn from his botched and derelict creation.[17] There are also hints in Hamm of Beckett's other mysterious petty gods or tyrants; an unhappy Murphy, tormented and immobilized, a poverty-stricken Mr Knott reduced to a single servant on the point of leaving, Pozzo, another master with an enslaved servant, or even a Godot, who, on arrival, turns out despotic and desperate, rather than benevolent. As well as being a 'ham' – or, as one critic suggests, *âme* (French for 'soul') – Hamm suggests 'hammer', especially in the light of critical suggestions that all three of the other character names may be derived from words meaning 'nail': Nell (*Nail*), Nagg (German *Nagel*) and Clov (French *Clou*), so that all the names make up a composite reference to the crucifixion.

These hints, however, fall short of allowing the spectator to make any kind of confident interpretation of the play on those grounds, partly because the play also insists the players are simply *onstage*. There are continual references to 'asides', to 'warming up for a last soliloquy' and to 'making an exit'. Hamm essays a Tragic Hero pose in his opening soliloquy, asking, with actorly gestures, 'Can there be misery [. . .] loftier than mine?' (*CDW* 93). As in *Godot*, the characters disconcertingly pre-empt audience responses; Clov turns his telescope on the audience at one stage and says 'I see . . . a multitude . . . in transports . . . of joy' (*CDW* 106), while Hamm remarks: 'This is deadly' and 'Not an underplot, I trust?' (*CDW* 130). As the tramps had to wait for Godot, so the characters of *Endgame* are constrained to remain by 'the dialogue' (*CDW* 121), doomed to re-enact it until the general public loses interest and the play's run, mercifully, comes to an end.

There is, thus, an uncomfortable meta-theatrical closeness between the predicament of *Endgame*'s characters and that of its actors. The actors play self-consciously theatrical characters who are doomed to perpetual re-enactment and imprisonment within the play until some external force decides otherwise. Hamm, we are to suppose, is simply kept onstage in his chair between performances, along with Nell and Nagg in their bins, covered up to keep the dust off, while the first action of the play is a ritual removal of the dustsheets, ready for yet another deadly performance: 'Finished, it's finished, nearly finished, it must be nearly finished' (*CDW* 93). We, as spectators, having shown up for an evening's theatre, are the inexorable forces demanding a performance; we are as implicated in this reluctant spectacle as the 'college of tyrants' that keeps the Unnamable churning out words. If all the world is a stage, then it is in no cheerful way.

The title of the play derives from a chess term, indicating the final phase of the game, when the board is almost empty. Of the phalanx of pieces aligned at the outset of the game, of the high hopes of the opening moves, almost nothing remains. Only some lowly residual pawn is left to protect the king. Hamm, red-faced in his wheelchair, moving little, suggests the Red King, who can move only one square at a time; Clov, nimbler, suggests a more mobile Red piece, perhaps, given his stumbling gait, the knight's L-shaped move. Hamm's game, perhaps originally imposing, is now 'nearly finished'. Beckett commented that Hamm's endgame is the game of a 'bad player', and sees him making 'a few senseless moves as only a bad player would. A good one would have given up long ago.'[18] The 'old endgame lost of old' (*CDW* 132) is life, and it is inevitably 'lost of old' because, no matter how skilfully the pieces are moved about the board during the game of chess, death will inevitably checkmate all manoeuvres.

In *Endgame*, no mysterious Godot may arrive and redeem the dramatis personae; they cannot even expect a visit from passers-by, or a messenger boy. No one at all waits in the wings of *Endgame*; only the pieces already on the board can engage with each other in the 'Bare interior. Grey light' (*CDW* 92) of their skull-room. The only potential visitor is an unwelcome one; with Clov's sighting of the distant child, there remains a vague, unresolved possibility that the boy may be another Clov come to serve Hamm. It may be that life does go on, despite appearances, and there is another game of chess still to be played. Beckett subtitled *Waiting for Godot* 'a tragicomedy', and this would also fit *Endgame*, but this time the tragicomedy dips towards the tragic end of the spectrum. True tragedy, of course, is not possible in the Beckett universe, where events never mean enough to qualify as genuinely tragic. *Endgame* is as near as Beckett gets to tragedy, and the monstrous soliloquizer Hamm, sufferer but also tormentor, as near as he gets to a tragic hero. We experience no catharsis, however, in a dramatic world in which 'nothing is as funny as unhappiness' (*CDW* 101).

KRAPP'S LAST TAPE TO *PLAY*

The stage plays of the late 1950s and early 1960s – *Krapp's Last Tape* (1958), *Happy Days* (1961) and *Play* (1963) – are, in comparison to *Godot* and *Endgame*, reduced in scale and dramatis personae, pointing ahead to the minimalism of the plays of the 1970s and 1980s. Essentially monological in their structure, each deals with an instance of isolated consciousness, although none of the three consists of a single voice speaking. While the previous plays have hinted at fissions of style, tone and persona within a single speaker (for instance, Hamm, Nagg and Pozzo's tendency to split off into narrators and actors within their speeches), it is the mid-period drama that establishes Beckettian monologue as complex and multiple, often consisting of a single voice splitting into several, to offer 'company' in an unresponsive and terminal world. As in Beckett's prose, monologue in his drama is never single – Krapp encounters the voices of his younger recorded self on his tape recorder, Winnie draws upon her 'classics' for company, while *Play*'s inquisitorial spotlight interlaces three

51

monologues into a single relay race of voices. If these plays make the monologue central, they also make it problematic. These plays consciously lean against Aristotelian notions of character and action, and retain some vestiges of the conventional play, but they also gesture ahead to the spare, scarcely human 'dramaticules' of the 1970s and 1980s.

Krapp's Last Tape

Krapp's Last Tape (1958) is a duet between a man and a tape recorder. An old man communes with a monologue he tape-recorded some three decades earlier, in which, having decided to relinquish love – ironically, the only experience the older, onstage Krapp finds of any value – he predicts for himself a brilliant future as a writer. The situation is intrinsically dramatic – an old man reviews his life, encounters, through technology, his past self and the decisions of that self, and thinks about his present plight. That the means of self-examination and confrontation is a tape recorder explains why Beckett's stage directions set the play 'in the future'. This is necessary for chronological plausibility, as the advent of home recording only began in the 1950s, and Krapp needed to be able to look back on a lifetime's worth of taped archives. The possibilities of the tape recorder fascinated Beckett from the time of his involvement with the BBC on the production of his 1957 radio play *All That Fall*. That fascination emerges in *Krapp's Last Tape* in the form of a medium that enables the storing and retrieval of a story or a selfhood, with each intonation, inflexion and nuance registered exactly, more faithful and more inexorable than memory, allowing the listener, as Krapp says, to 'be again' (*CDW* 223).

The 69-year-old Krapp onstage is clownish, a bored, bitter, short-sighted old dipsomaniac, with a vaudevillean passion for bananas and a cracked old-man voice. We hear, on the other hand, the voice of the 39-year-old Krapp on the tape he listens to, a *'strong* [. . .] *rather pompous'* voice, which tells us the younger Krapp is 'sound as a bell' and intellectually 'at the [. . .] crest of the wave' (*CDW* 217). The effect is eerie, as of a *Doppelgänger*, or, given that the younger Krapp has in turn been listening to a tape recorded when he was in his late

52

twenties, a whole series of Krapps. Andrew Kennedy remarks that 'it is like seeing a face endlessly reflected between two mirrors'.[19] The various Krapps share only their constipation, weaknesses for drink and bananas, and their sneering at their younger selves, but seem more like separate strangers than stages in the life of the same man. As the 39-year-old Krapp says of his younger self, 'Hard to believe I was ever that young whelp. The voice! Jesus! And the aspirations!' (*CDW* 218). The situation is both comical and uncanny, the confrontations between a relatively rich past and an impoverished present, and the pained encounter between mutually strange versions of a self. Neither is it a coincidence that Krapp is a writer, or a failed writer, by profession, because his activities throughout the play are noticeably authorial. He narrates himself onto tape, then, to listen to what he wants, he winds forward and back, skips, repeats; essentially, he edits his recordings, and thereby himself.

After some initial semi-senile clowning, the chief business of the play is Krapp's listening to three, rather fragmented, taped passages, interlinked by patterns of imagery – light and dark, separation and fusion – and a preoccupation with the feminine. These episodes are listed in his ledger as 'Mother at rest at last', 'Memorable equinox' and 'Farewell to love', laconically listed alongside 'Slight improvement in bowel condition' (*CDW* 217), in a way that recalls the unhelpful summaries of *Mercier and Camier*. The first episode, narrating Krapp's mother's death, is notable for its already ingrained habit of extreme self-exclusion and detachment. Krapp, not at the deathbed, sits outside by a canal watching his mother's window, 'wishing she were gone' (*CDW* 219); there is a self-preening pedantry in his account, and in his use of the arcane word 'viduity', which the older Krapp has to go and look up.

The second passage, the 'Memorable equinox', is heard only in snatches; Krapp's interest in it is only casually curious. As he had forgotten the meaning of 'viduity', the 'Memorable equinox', ironically, has been completely forgotten by the older Krapp. The equinox in question was apparently of note for a mysterious vision into the heart of things the younger Krapp had, on a stereotypically Romantic stormy pier. The purport of this equinoctial vision, greeted by Krapp-at-39 as 'the whole thing. The vision at last' (*CDW*, 220), is never made clear, as the older Krapp becomes bored with the younger and fast-forwards continually. We know only that the 'storm and night with the light of the understanding and the fire' and making some kind of aesthetic terms with 'the dark I have always struggled to keep under' (*CDW* 222) leaves the young Krapp pregnant with the promise of a great literary work, never achieved, or if achieved, never recognized. Only seventeen copies of this 'magnum opus' were sold.

Linked to the 'Memorable equinox' is the episode that so fascinates the older Krapp that he listens to it twice. In contrast to the visionary diction of the previous passage, comically truncated by the bored older Krapp, 'Farewell to love' has a becalmed rhythmic poise that almost imitates the gentle drifting of the punt in which he and his lover agree that it is 'hopeless' and 'no good going on' (*CDW* 223). Even as they agree to part at Krapp's instigation, the episode is an intensely erotic idyll, unique in Beckett's usually Swiftian treatment of sex. Krapp at 69, solitary, embittered and impotent, savours this elegiac tale of lost love, with its muted sensuality, its tender cadences and its intimations of intimacy even in farewell. It is all too ironic a contrast to his present deprived reality of 'the sour cud and the iron stool' and the 'bony old ghost of a whore' who visits him (*CDW* 222). Although he rips the tape off the machine and records a ferocious riposte – 'Be again, be again. [. . .] All that old misery. [. . .] Once wasn't enough for you' – a repetition of the 'Farewell to love' ends the play. This time, however, the engrossed Krapp lets the tape run on to the end: 'Perhaps my best years are gone. When there was a chance of happiness. But I wouldn't want them back. Not with the fire in me now' (*CDW* 223).

The irony lies in the broken older Krapp's near-parodic re-enactment of the scene, caressing his substitute object, the tape recorder, bending over it with his hand on it, as his younger self bent over the woman. Yet another irony sees the voice of the younger Krapp apparently mocking the elder across time. The old Krapp 'burning to be gone' hears the younger self saying he wouldn't want back his 'best years', 'when there was a chance of happiness': 'Not with the fire in me now.' For the arrogant young would-be artist who re-corded it, rejecting love in favour of art is an affirmation of strength and purpose. But for the embittered old failure listening to it, motionless in his dark den, it represents the entirety of human feeling, erotic love and connectedness to others, which now, ironically, he has come to value. By repeating the scene and ending the play with it, Beckett satirically undermines the force of Krapp's denial of feeling, and underscores the value of what he has lost. The inexorable voice from the past, preserved on tape in eerie nuance, is both more and less moving the second time around: more, because it is an elegy for fruitless repudiation; less, because a last amour is reduced to a recorded echo.

Happy Days

Happy Days, written in English in 1961, seems at first glance atypically jovial for a Beckett play. Even setting aside its improbably cheery title, Beckett gives his female lead a highly theatrical voice – endlessly garrulous, perky, confiding, resil-ient – very different from the austere purity of language the spectator has come to expect. The play does, however, more familiarly, offer one of the most surreal and recognizably Beckettian stage images; a woman buried first up to her waist, then her neck, in sand. The scenario is arguably the most surreal in all Beckett's drama, not just because of the Dali-esque weirdness of a woman buried in a mound, but because of the unflagging and desperate attempts she makes to present herself as an unexceptional middle-class married woman – one critic calls her an 'English suburban Edna Everage'[20] – in a manner at once grotesque and poignant. In this, Winnie is what Paul Lawley calls a 'virtuoso of the inconsequential'.[21] Painfully aware of her physical situation, she remains unaware of its absurdity, continuing to address herself to the task of self-construction with sprightly tenacity. An appalling tension is generated between increasingly desperate stage image and buoyant chatter.

Happy Days has been read as Beckett's savage satire on the polite suburban values of his class from which he dissented, and certainly it is not difficult to see the play as an acerbic take on marriage stereotypes: an unresponsive, slouching, verbally bullied husband with boater, paper and saucy postcard, and a cosily iron-willed wife, armoured in cliché, consoled by possessions, going through her circumscribed daily round, in a torrent of chatter about 'happy days'. Yet, as always with Beckett, the play pre-empts disquieted audience responses, by having Winnie tell the story of 'the last human kind to stray this way', a couple who stare disbelievingly at her half-buried form, and ask 'What's the idea? [. . .] stuck up to her diddies in the bleeding ground [. . .] What's it meant to mean?' (*CDW* 156).

If she hardly resembles the Job-like complainers of other Beckett works, Winnie is still subjected to the same privations of isolation, immobility and enthralment to the commands of an external force, in this case a bell. Optimistic to the end, she ends as a kind of comic version of the Unnamable's final panicky 'I can't go on, I'll go on', still counting her unimaginably small mercies. Almost any of her speeches could be spoken in an ordinary suburban setting; the incongruity of *Happy Days* is that Winnie's chirpy platitudes are spoken under hellish conditions that are never explained. There are elements reminiscent of *Endgame*; the depopulated earth, ferocious light and heat, the spontaneous combustion of the parasol and Winnie's fear of being 'charred to a black cinder' (*CDW* 154) suggest another post-nuclear scenario. Also like *Endgame*, however, is the insistence that Winnie's predicament is simply being onstage, responding to the prompter's bell, steeling herself to her uncomfortable part ('begin, Winnie') immobilized under unchanging artificial light, improvising on her collection of props – toothbrush, mirror, spectacles and revolver – confident that, although her parasol burns and her mirror breaks during her performance, both will be replaced by the morrow, as though by a theatrical properties manager. The metatheatricality is reminiscent of *Endgame*, but, whereas Hamm has Clov as the other half of his double act and audience, Winnie's sense of the audience is frequently just a threatening sense of being observed, and her attempts to set up a duet with Willie, her husband, are failures. Again, Beckett takes a basic theatrical situation – the repeatability of the theatrical run, the caretaking function of the invisible backstage functionaries, the predicament of an actor trapped in a role – and both literalizes them and makes them metaphors for 'going on'.

Words are properties, too, resources for survival just like the contents of the capacious bag through which she rummages, Malone-like, in Act I. As for many Beckett characters, words for Winnie are not just instruments of self-expression, but almost material objects available for manœuvring and deployment in her task of survival, like Molloy's sucking stones. Terry Eagleton is right when he says that Beckett's language often resembles 'chunks of shopsoiled cliché to be fingered like worry beads, reach-me-down rags to be tossed to and fro, crumbling bits of proverb to be stored away like mouldy sweets'.[22] The analogy is especially apt in the case of Winnie, as her words are derived words, to an even greater extent than that to which the words of any speaker are derived. Quoting – usually inaccurately – and alluding to the famous words of others are her most important techniques for facing down the irremediable: 'That is what I find so wonderful, a part remains, of one's classics, to help one through the day' (*CDW* 164). 'Fear no more the heat o' the sun', she quotes, as Willie crawls into the shade she cannot reach. She greets yet another day of blinding illumination and heat with Milton's 'Hail, holy light', and, putting on lipstick, she mangles Romeo's speech over the drugged Juliet: 'Ensign crimson [. . .] Pale flag' (*CDW* 142). Of course Winnie's ensign of beauty is cosmetic in origin and her Romeo spends the entire play ignoring her, so that it is ironically appropriate that this faded Juliet speaks only a mutilated remnant of Romeo's speech.

Winnie as speaker is subject to imperatives similar to those to which all Beckett voices are forced to conform: the compulsion to go on saying words as long as there are any, and the necessity of trying to articulate some kind of selfhood. Her inappropriately buoyant chatter and ritualized habits thus appear to be an attempt to domesticate the strange, purgatorial scenario in which she is, literally, planted. Her frequent recourse to a 'sweet old style' of speech seems to indicate she is seeking 'semantic succour' similar to that of Watt in Mr Knott's house. However, her wholesale derivation of words from other sources continually hampers her attempts to constitute herself within language, pointed up by her perverse use of the phrase 'happy days' to designate her struggling existence. Her use of language seems mere lip-service, the adherence to a formula of ritualized words, as when she directs herself to 'Pray your old prayer, Winnie' (CDW 159).

A bleak realization of the inherent inadequacy of language punctuates the determined cheerfulness of her monologue with a moment of resigned sadness: 'Words fail, there are times when even they fail [. . .]' (CDW 162). Winnie, unable to wrest words to her will, appears almost entirely to be spoken *through*, to be a passive mouthpiece for the rags of erudition. The mound that so encroaches upon her already limited freedom indicates the linguistic and cultural debris that, by its accumulation, threatens to bury her completely, rather than build up into a way of speaking her self. Winnie is staged as a portmanteau for the 'classics' of an exhausted civilization, whose accumulated knowledge has no relevance to her absurd situation. That the mangled repetition of this knowledge becomes part of a ritual that also involves hair combing and teeth inspections heightens the irony, just as Cartesian rationalism is debased to mathematical games in the trilogy. Winnie's monologue, thus, rather than enabling her to construct herself within language, puts her in the position of experiencing herself only fragmentarily, in the interstices of the 'derived' verbal material that issues from her lips, and that seems at times to be almost independent of her: 'There is so little one can say, one says it all [. . .] all one can' (CDW 161).

Play

Play, written in English in 1962–3, offers an eerie combination of Protestant Hell, with characters condemned to repeat eternally the story of their sordid sins on earth, and a culmination of the speech-as-interrogation trope that has featured in several previous Beckett texts. In several senses, *Play* offers a logical extension of some of the grotesqueries of *Happy Days*. Where Winnie is increasingly confined in her mound in blazing light, *Play*'s three characters, a man and two women involved in a sordid love triangle, are literally 'potted' in identical large urns on a darkened set evocative of a

Dantean Purgatory. Where Winnie is extravagantly expressive in her improvisation, they, *'impassive throughout'* (CDW 308), repeat a set text in a monotone. Winnie's performance is controlled by a tyrannical bell; the urn-enclosed shades have as their 'unique inquisitor' a spotlight that provokes their speech, swivelling from one face to another. The dramatic importance of the movements of the spotlight means the *Play* is really a quartet rather than a trio. As so often in Beckett's later drama, technology takes on a menacing stage personality. The privileged spotlight initiates the action and controls it throughout, like an inhuman conductor conducting solos, arias and choruses. Players recite their lines only when their purgatorial privacy has been invaded by the light, although there is never any sign that an interrogator is listening, let alone paying attention, as the swivelling spotlight often abandons a face in mid-narrative, even in mid-sentence. Without the metatheatrical operations of the light there would be no words and no play, but its procedure is indubitably a form of torture, working on its imprisoned victims; as in *Endgame*, we as spectators here to see the 'play' are necessarily in collusion with it.

Set in some post-mortem environment akin to the setting of *The Unnamable*, the three urn-bound heads, their faces *'so lost to age and aspect as to seem part of the urns'* (CDW 308), converge on a common topic. Throughout their radically interrupted speeches, as the spotlight swivels from one face to another, the spectator gradually makes out a banal story of wife, husband and mistress. W1 and W2, wife and mistress, tell their contiguous stories in tones of elegant banality grossly at odds with their current depleted condition. 'Judge then of my astonishment when one fine morning, as I was sitting stricken in the morning room [. . .]', W1 begins, while W2, for her part, resorts to her butler to face off the threat of the other woman: 'Fearing she was about to offer me violence, I rang for Erskine and had her shown out' (CDW 309). M, the man, a vain professional, a preening adept of the clichés of smug penitence, cuts a less fine rhetorical figure, his narrative interrupted by attacks of hiccups as well as the departure of the spotlight. What exactly occurs to terminate this speeded-up drawing-room melodrama, all butlers, hired detectives and rancorous exits, and to land its protagonists in their current situation, remains unclear.

Here they are, however, endlessly rehearsing their tawdry tale for eternity, none knowing the others are nearby, but supposing them to remain 'up there' alive. The middle section of *Play* sees the three begin to focus on their current situation, rather than their shared past, and move from past to present tense. They cope with their present variously. W1 screams at the light as though it is sexually violating her ('Get off me'), or, at other times, as though it is a lover who may 'weary' of her, and wonders what she must do to satisfy it: 'Is it that I do not tell the truth, is that it, that some day somehow I may tell the truth at last and then no more light at last, for the truth?' (*CDW* 313). W2 is sure the light knows she is doing her best, but suspects, rather hopefully, that she is becoming a little unhinged. M imagines the two women drawn together in their common grief at losing him, as he had once fantasized of having them both together – 'such fantasies' – the women disappointing him by their lack of complicity with his desires. The past, he now declares, is 'just play', and wonders if he will ever be able to look back with similar detachment on his current condition: 'When will all this have been . . . just play?' (*CDW* 313).

The final third of *Play* sees an exact repeat of the opening third, as the actors obey a stage direction that reads '*Repeat play*' (*CDW* 317). The spectator, second time around, however, is of course encountering a new work. Whereas a first viewing involves frantic piecing together of clues and attempting to render intelligible the baleful monotones of the urned heads, the second encounter allows the comprehension of hints and unities, and gives birth to the terrible understanding that we may be simply eavesdropping on the torments of the damned, that these three are condemned to repeat their tale for all eternity. A repetition of the play also allows us to grasp the unrelenting nature of this hell. Previous Beckett works have also employed versions of this device of complex repetition: Moran's journey recapitulates Molloy's; *Godot*'s two acts suggest an endless series of failed meetings; Krapp's 'Farewell to love' recording strikes a very different note the second time he plays it; Winnie's increasingly appalling circumstances make the chirpy armour of cliché of Act II still more terrible than that of Act I. The exact repetition of *Play* removes any sense that this is an apocalyptic kind of hell, where punishment is once and done for ever, but a more chilling affair entirely, with the necessity to go on saying identical words with no end ever in sight, and no 'truth' to call a halt, for the insatiable curiosity of the audience. We are also, as so often in Beckett plays, afraid we may be subjected to an endless series of acts; will we ever be allowed to leave and get back out into the light? Beckett posits no end, merely a series of repetitions to this chillingly dehumanized sex farce, with only the dimming of the light during the repeat in some productions suggesting that each repetition may grow closer to the darkness for which W1 yearns.

One of Beckett's primary innovations in his drama from *Godot* to *Play* is first to question the formal structure he inherited and that dramatists of previous generations had felt compelled to respect, and, secondly, to offer a representation of reality that recognizes and inscribes the formlessness of existence without feeling the need to tidy it into neat artistic compartments, categories or models, according to his credo that the artist should find a form that 'accommodates the mess'.[23] Beckett's plays are metatheatrical, in that they both are theatre and comment upon theatre; when read, though more forcibly in performance, they challenge the conventional contract between play and spectator or reader, denying as they do any suspension of disbelief. While his engagement with the 'well-made' play is at its most confrontational in *Godot* and *Endgame*, the later, briefer dramas tend towards a rewriting of the stage monologue – traditionally the playwright's tool for confirming and revealing individual identity – and turn it instead into a tool that disperses, when it does not actually destabilize, the individual. In this endemic mistrust of the adequacy of subjectivity, Beckett holds faith with his earlier insights in *Proust* that the 'creation of the world did not take place once and for all time, but takes place every day, as we forge new compromises between ourselves and our environment' (*PTD* 19). This need daily to invent the world is taken to frightening extremes in *Godot* and *Endgame*, where every day is like the next, where no sense of continuum allows characters to link today to yesterday, and in *Krapp's Last Tape, Happy Days* and *Play*, in which various fictions of identity are essayed, and the past is continually evoked via various forms of mechanical repetition, but never add up to any adequate form of identity. These dramas are 'just ... play', but the object of their ritual re-enactment of situations is not fun, but defence against a world Beckett's speakers cannot comprehend or accept.

4

'Ghost rooms': The Late
Theatre

Beckett's 1969 playlet *Breath* lasts approximately thirty-five
seconds, and dispenses entirely with actors and words. The
complete text of the play, including all stage directions,
consists of a terse paragraph of instructions. On a stage
scattered with 'miscellaneous rubbish', a faint recorded birth-
cry, a single breath in and out, and a death-cry, are heard, to
the accompaniment of a light that brightens momentarily and
fades again to darkness. Beckett told his first biographer that
'the best possible play is one in which there are no actors, only
the text' and *Breath* is the realization of this somewhat chilling
vision.[1] Its brevity – and the fact that it was offered by Beckett
as an opener to Kenneth Tynan's 'erotic revue' *Oh! Calcutta!* –
suggests a final epigrammatic comment on the human condition.[2] If it had been a last play – especially one that appears to
cock a snook at the richness of theatre history, by a writer who
would win the Nobel Prize later the same year – *Breath* would
have appeared a bleakly final reduction of Beckett's lifetime of
writing about deprivation in all its forms, whether material,
emotional or cultural: a play itself deprived of any of the
resources of art. However, in a writing career that still had two
decades to run, *Breath*'s 'cosmic yawn', as one critic dubs it, a
literal and metaphorical last gasp, exhibits an exhaustion and
boredom with theatre that is nowhere evident in the richly
innovative short plays still to come during the 1970s and
1980s.[3] All these later dramas share with *Breath* is Beckett's
interest in how much does *not* have to happen onstage for a
play to have dramatic potential, and in exploring the minimum
necessary to convey human-ness on stage.

Beckett's plays of the 1970s and 1980s embark on an entirely new dramatic mode, both in comparison to his own previous work, and in relation to theatre in the West. Often described as 'minimal' – a term usually associated with geometry and abstraction in the visual arts – they attempt to do more and more with ever less material. From *Come and Go* (1965) onwards, none of them takes up more than ten pages or so of printed text or more than forty minutes of performance time. Brevity is one of the unifying features of this group of fragmentary, generically homeless texts, which are best designated by a term Beckett himself first coined in the subtitle to *Come and Go*: 'dramaticule' (literally 'playlet', with intimations of reticule, portability, smallness). There is evidence that Beckett conceived the miniature play as a genre of its own; he collected a number of late dramatic texts under the title *Catastrophe et autres dramaticules*. Enoch Brater aptly dubs them 'chamber plays', for their capacity to translate proscenium arch into intimate performance space.[4] What they lack in physical scale – they famously contain as many stage directions as there are lines to be said, and the playing space and physical freedom allotted to the player becomes ever more cramped – is compensated for in an almost hallucinatory intensity. Bare stage spaces offer the spectator a palette of gradations of grey, from which voices elaborate dislocation and unease. Highly conscious of their status as theatre, these plays focus on performance as a mode of self-consciousness, in relation to Beckett's creatures' attempts to represent themselves, to bear witness to their existences through their narratives, often on stages that suggest scenes of judgement or metamorphosis.

Besides their extreme brevity, one of the most intriguing aspects of the late plays is their engagement with the feminine in an œuvre that, with few exceptions, has been an exclusively, almost parodically, male preserve. To some extent, this is due to Beckett's enduring fascination with the quality of the actress Billie Whitelaw's voice in the 1964 Old Vic production of *Play*, and his resolve to write a drama for her. The resulting 'Whitelaw trilogy', *Not I* (1972), *Footfalls* (1976) and *Rockaby* (1981), offers, along with an increasing concision and minimalism, a preoccupation with loss, fragmentation and an intrinsic *manque-à-être* represented within the plays via tenuous, often

64

truncated, ambiguously there female presences. Such presences are much at odds with the fragmentary, but still recognizable, female characters of *Happy Days* and *All That Fall*, or the exuberant female stereotypes of the early fiction. These dramaticules provide an apotheosis of absence in their staging of female non-subjects, literal 'not I's, whose lack of subject status provides a discordant counterpoint to the monologic structures of the theatre. The woman-centred late plays have received considerable attention from feminist critics, though there is little consensus on whether the inscription of the feminine as attenuated figurations of lack in these dramas constitutes a male-authored figuration of female powerlessness and absence, or an indictment of the unitary subject and its representation.[5] Male-centred plays of the period, such as *That Time*, have often been deemed somewhat lacklustre in comparison.

Semi-corporeal indefiniteness and frequent bodily truncation, added to the dimness and ambiguousness of the playing space of the late plays, and a repeated recourse to ritualized movement and speech, have suggested to many critics that the twilight space inhabited by these faint visual ghosts is not entirely of this world. Keir Elam has influentially argued that all Beckett's late drama, in so far as it is 'about' anything other than its own increasingly skeletal resources, deals essentially with death. The speaker of *A Piece of Monologue* insists there can be no other topic: 'Never but the one matter. The dead and the gone. The dying and the going' (*CDW* 429). Many of the late plays' speakers are aged or post-mortem 'dead heads' (the French title Beckett gave to a collection of his short fiction in 1967), lit against darkness, set apart from centre stage as though in a geometrically tangential relationship to whatever of life remains to them.

The frequent stage direction that the figures be played by actors rendered 'as alike in appearance as possible' suggests chillingly a kind of Limbo or Purgatory in which individual features are rendered hellishly alike, muted into compulsively narrating shades, for whom, even if 'little is left to tell', as *Ohio Impromptu* has it, that 'little' must still be revolved and repeated in increasingly minimal, reticent and negative narratives. The likelihood of *Not I* (1972) having been influenced by

65

Gustave Doré's illustrations to Dante's *Inferno* has been noted by many. However, the Dantean atmosphere and infernal references extend throughout the late drama, allowing us to imagine the dramaticules taking place in some deathly or hellish simultaneity, narrating themselves in a terse version of Dante's *Inferno*, side by side but unseeing, imagining themselves alone, like the urned heads in *Play*.

Genre is subjected to severe stress in the late drama, as it is in Beckett's late prose. Drama, narrative and poetry seem to bleed into one another, and the 'play' frequently seems to be on the verge of turning into something more akin to a performance poem, or staged prose that cannot be seen as 'dramatic' in any conventional sense. If *Godot* was simultaneously hailed and reviled by its early critics for verging on an 'anti-play', then Beckett's late work in the theatre is perhaps post-drama. While all the late plays could be described in terms of the title of one of their number, *A Piece of Monologue*, these are monologues distressed and interrupted by what one critic calls the 'degree of synecdochal risk taken to convey the minimum necessary to convey human-ness'.[6] Those familiar with Beckett's early and mid-period drama are already accustomed to various complex forms of fragmentation of the body operating against the metaphysics of presence the theatre necessarily enlists; the superannuated amputees in their dustbins in *Endgame*, *Happy Days'* Winnie immured in her mound, the urn-bound trio of *Play*. However, in the dramas of the 1970s and 1980s, we are confronted, as Andrew Kennedy outlines, 'with further and radical instances of dramatic "lessness": miniature monodramas that pursue a principle of self-diminishment, that is, the self moving towards existential and verbal extinction'.[7]

All these late plays lean against the soliloquy as we know it from Shakespeare onward, as *How It Is* leans against the Miltonic and Dantean epic, and as Beckett's earlier drama depends for many of its effects on subtle implicit comparisons with more conventional theatre. Beckett's plays of the 1950s and 1960s continually worked in terms of warping the logic of the well-made play, cyclical in contrast to conventional linear action, offering an immobilized protagonist rather than an action hero, and jerky asyntactical rhythms rather than the norms of naturalistic stage dialogue. In the late plays, Beckett completely overturns the Aristotelian notion of 'character' as complete in body, capable in speech, conquering time with action. Rather than making revelations, they operate via truncation, repetition, concealment and circularity; in all, the protagonists appear strangely onstage, 'not quite there', 'slightly off centre', asking questions about theatrical power and authority. The mode of the 1970s and 1980s plays, in their minimalist and interiorized adaptation of the pronoun drama of *The Unnamable*, elaborates 'the non-self in a no-longer soliloquy'.[8]

NOT I and *THAT TIME*

One critic comments that it is difficult to tell whether *Not I* is primarily spectacle or literature.[9] Written in English in 1972, this fifteen-minute play presents the spectator with a characteristically bare stage. At one side, stands a shrouded, silent, mostly immobile Auditor, who at times suggests a priest-figure listening to a penitent in the confessional, a courtroom judge listening to a witness's testimony, or, it has been suggested, a goading prompter in a purgatorial rehearsal. In contrast to this mute giant of 'indeterminable sex' there is, upstage right, suspended eight feet above the stage, a disembodied spot-lit mouth, dementedly jabbering to itself in the darkness.

Mouth gives birth to verbal statements as alarmingly fragmented as herself. Certainly her utterances form nothing so organized or coherent as a sentence. The play text is a tissue of ellipses, reminiscent of the fragmentary blurts of text of *How It Is*. The audience experiences a performance as an almost unintelligible verbal onslaught, as the curtain rises on Mouth's mutterings, which crescendo gradually into a periodic anguished scream, then settle again into a rapid monotone drone. Frantically hurrying forth speech, correcting itself, compulsively doubling back to repeat, amplify or deny, Mouth's narrative tells the story of an elderly female vagrant, orphaned since birth ('so no love . . . spared that') who has spent her seventy wretched years chiefly in muteness, apart from episodes, 'once or twice a year . . . always winter some strange reason . . . the long evenings . . . hours of darkness,' when she is overcome with a 'sudden urge to . . . tell . . .' (*CDW* 379).

The chief peculiarity of Mouth's tattered narrative is its internal drama of the first-person pronoun, at whose potentialities Beckett has already hinted in *The Unnamable*. There are a multiplicity of interpretations of the title. 'Not I' is also 'not aye', and operates as a kind of dramatic negation of Molly Bloom's famous 'yes' soliloquy. Unlike Joyce's reverence for 'yes', Mouth's narrative consists of negations – 'no matter', 'no love', 'no moon', 'no screaming', 'no response', interspersed with a litany of 'not', 'never' and 'nothing'. Mouth's chief concern within the play, according to Beckett's unusually direct note to the play text, is her 'vehement refusal to relinquish third person' (*CDW* 375). Her desperate struggle to avoid saying 'I' is signalled by four moments of crisis in her monologue, which momentarily becomes a dialogue with some inaudible prompting or coercing voice: 'what? . . who? . . no! . . she!' At these frantic swerves away from self-acknowledgement, from grammatical ownership of what is presumably her own miserable story, the cowled figure of the Auditor, who may perhaps also be her inquisitor, makes one of its minimal gestures of what Beckett's note tells us is 'helpless compassion' (*CDW* 375); essentially, Auditor shrugs.

Mouth's emphatic insistence on 'she' is an implicit rejection of the personal pronoun that threatens to violate her insistent third-person narration, and to transform her into a unwilling autobiographer. Her repeated refusal to identify with the first-person singular suggests that self-recognition equates to self-mutilation or even self-immolation. It is as though the play's poetics of negation, Mouth's refusal of the pronominal bond, fragments the body it should link to, resulting in the disconcertingly negated and splintered stage image. She will speak of the wretched life only as lived by another, in the past. However, the more Mouth denies herself, insists on her own non-subjectivity, the more she betrays her tortured self-consciousness as self-reflexive stage subject. She talks about her 'sudden urge to . . . tell', 'the beam' of light that illuminates her, the curious eyes of spectators witnessing her distressing bursts of speech in a public place. (In her narrative, theatre has become public toilet, a Beckettian joke more reminiscent of the end of *Murphy* than any of his more recent work.) Willy-nilly, her attempts at self-evasion become a viciously public self-exhibition, with the spectator scripted in, as so often in these late Dantean dramas, as a heartless voyeur.

Yet, as in all Beckett's late drama, the tenuous 'plot' is of secondary impact only. It is the visual impact that commands attention in performance. 'I am not unduly concerned with intelligibility,' Beckett told Jessica Tandy, who played Mouth in the New York premiere. 'I hope the piece may work on the nerves of its audience, not its intellect.'[10] The speed at which the monologue is spoken certainly inhibits any detailed comprehension of the details of Mouth's narrative; Billie Whitelaw, who played Mouth in the first London production at the Royal Court, practised speed-speaking using the stopwatches on television sports events. The experience remains primarily visceral, the effect hypnotic. In production one is almost overwhelmed by the image of the mouth – disembodied, suspended in space, throbbing with a constant pulsation of lips, tongue and teeth – hanging in the middle of otherwise empty theatre space.

Certainly the arresting visual image, wordless giant in mute contrast to jabbering orifice, seems to have been the originary idea for the play. It suggests the dislocation of surrealist painters like Magritte, or the visually haunting images of Bunuel's *Un chien andalou*. Beckett himself suggested different stories as to how he had arrived at the idea of the play, telling James Knowlson in 1974 that the idea had emerged from seeing Caravaggio's *Decollation of St John* during a 1971 visit to Malta; he also told Jessica Tandy that the seed of the play came from seeing, on a holiday in North Africa, a djellaba-covered figure leaning against a wall in a pose suggesting intense listening. To yet other people, Beckett suggested an earlier source for the play in a series of old crone-figures with whom he was familiar from his Irish childhood. Whatever its source, the shockingly disembodied mouth onstage is a curiously hypnotic and polyvalent icon. Its spasmodic movements eerily suggest aspects of the events she narrates – it is the 'godforsaken hole' through which she was conceived and from which she is expelled into the world, which experiences isolated instances of unpleasurable copulation, defecation or menstrual flow; it suggests the mouth, which gives birth to uncontrollable speech, the eye, which weeps, and the 'I', which is denied. The mouth, severed from its usual bodily context and meaning, becomes a kind of blank onto which the audience can project any number of meanings – over the course of the brief play it plays the roles of vagina, uterus, anus, mouth proper, eye and even ear. Even as it is fractured in the very attempt to deny its own existence in terms of disowning its life story, it suggests aspects of that life.[11]

Not I has been read as a case study in psychological 'splitting off', with Mouth as a schizoid personality. But it has also been read in Dantean terms, with Mouth suffering afterlife torment. Keir Elam suggests a specific reference to the *Inferno*'s final and most terrible Circle IX, in which Dante encounters the talking heads of traitors showing above the surface of the frozen lake of Coccytus, their bodies invisible below the ice.[12] One of these reluctant spectacles refuses to tell his name to Dante even when physically tormented by him, but is addressed by his neighbour by the name *Bocca*, literally 'Mouth'. It seems plausible that Beckett's Mouth has her genesis in Dante's *Bocca*, helpless and garrulous, refusing to admit to his identity, upbraided by the inhumane poet-spectator. Hélène L. Baldwin reads *Not I* as 'the *Inferno* pared down to a twelve-minute recital of sin by a single mouth which refuses to admit personal guilt and responsibility'.[13] Others have pointed out striking similarities with Gustave Doré's well-known illustration of the scene in which Dante and Virgil approach the talking traitor-ous heads, in which both poets are robed in black, like the Auditor. However, while the Auditor gestures in 'helpless compassion', the audience takes the part of the pitiless Dante and the punishing God, compelling with a watching eye endless rehearsals of infernal or purgatorial torment, as the theatre situation forces Mouth to recite her own evasive damnation-narrative in performance after performance. If she can avoid the 'I', she cannot similarly evade the 'eye' of the spectator.

Written in 1974–5, *That Time* is a kind of companion piece to *Not I*, to which it is adjacent chronologically. Presenting, with characteristic economy, a severed head with *'long flaring white hair as if seen from above outspread'* (*CDW* 388), which operates simultaneously as character, prop and stage set, it reverses the dramatic situation of its sibling play. Where Mouth talked, in *That Time* the iconic figure is a listener. (Beckett would never allow the two plays to be staged on a double bill together as he thought they were too self-consciously cut from the same texture, and certainly it seems likely that the more muted *That Time* would suffer by the comparison.) *That Time*'s disembodied head hovers ten feet above stage level off-centre. Like a surrealist image, its disembodiment remains disturbingly unexplained, but the oddly *'outspread'* hair suggests Listener's *'old white face'* is lying on a pillow, possibly on his deathbed, being revisited by aspects of his ruined and half-extinguished selfhood.

Listener is assailed by three voices – which we are informed by the stage directions are *'his own'* (*CDW* 388) - 'coming to him from both sides and above', each taunting him with fragments of stories from his past, of lonely un-Wordsworthian childhood, of an exiled adulthood and an old age spent in 'fear of ejection' from public places of shelter from the rain. The utterances of the three voices are symmetrically arranged, appearing in systematic triplets, divided into three balanced sections by the two ten-second pauses:

ACB ACB ACB CAB
CBA CBA CBA BCA
BAC BAC BAC BAC

During the two periods of silence between the story fragments, Listener's amplified breath fills the theatre and his eyes open and fix on the audience in supplication. There is no relief, no release, no denouement. What remains of the past is only remnants of what might once have been a coherent memory or a unified selfhood, now 'making up talk breaking up two or more talking to himself being together that way' (*CDW* 393). There is only a lonely trinity of isolated fragments offering no resolution or Wordsworthian tranquillity of memory.

Besides borrowing heavily from previous Beckett writings, *That Time*, it has been suggested, takes its title from Shakespeare's Sonnet 73, 'That time of year you may'st in me behold', with which it shares an autumnal, nostalgic and bleakly liminal atmosphere of yellow leaves, sunset, twilight and preoccupation with 'Death's second self, that seals all up in rest'. Like the television play ... *but the clouds* ... from the following year, which quotes a couplet from Yeats's 'The Tower', *That Time* gains some of its effects by leaning its 'tottering and muttering' frame against the prior text, subverting and muting its theme of imminent death strengthening love. While Shakespeare triumphs over time in the immortality of verse, Beckett's fugue disintegrates into silence and darkness. *That Time* also offers a muted and contracted version of *Krapp's Last Tape*, dispensing with the cumbrous technology that has formed the realistic occasion for Krapp's self-confrontation. Here, the voices A, B and C differ in that each owes its existence, shape, desires to a different moment in time, and are not mediated by technology, merely the elegiac Proustian recognition that the self over time is different but the same.

FOOTFALLS and ROCKABY

After the fragmented images of *Not I* and *That Time*, it is something of a relief to see a recognizable, and relatively realistic, complete figure onstage, as we do in both the brief, cyclic, sibling dramas, *Footfalls* (1976) and *Rockaby* (1981). In *Footfalls*, an isolated woman, with *'dishevelled grey hair'*, costumed like a ghost in a tattered cobweb, paces a premeditated path from right to left like one of Dante's damned. *Rockaby* has as its protagonist a *'prematurely old'* woman in mourning black and jet beads, and as its only stage prop a rocking chair in which she sits, transfixed by the pitiless light of a cold lunar glare and the sound of her own voice speaking a death-dealing lullaby. However, the fullness of the staged figure is no retreat from the pronounced anti-naturalism of *Not I* and *That Time*, as these subsequent plays arguably move still further into ever subtler fugues of denial, absence and repeated negativity, as well as an increasingly destabilized consistency of selfhood.

Footfalls, a play of exactly calibrated dimness and faintness of effect, uses stage lighting to retrench the acting area severely to a metre-wide space on which nine measured paces are taken. This focuses attention on the clearly audible rhythmic pad that constitutes the post-subjective, and possibly post-mortem, world of its protagonist, May, and the invisible mother-figure with whom she duets. In *Rockaby*, the seated Woman rocking herself into death forms a bizarre kinetic Whistler's Mother, in rhythmic counterpoint to her own recorded voice, eerily coming to resemble the image created by her inner monologue. Both plays feature an obsessive, ritualistic, to-and-fro movement, whether pacing or rocking, which accompanies and acts as a contrapuntal accompaniment to the verbal 'revolving ... it all' (*CDW* 400). Mary A. Doll has influentially read the walking and rocking of these plays as threshold rituals, by which the profane is rendered sacred, ghosts walk and rhythmic mantras can propel the self across the threshold of death.[14] Furthermore, in a startling movement away from the tightly defined parodic Cartesian male models of selfhood of the earlier prose, both plays offer variations on what Mary Bryden calls 'abstracted scenarios of self-sharing between women'.[15]

The rhythmic footfalls of the walking woman, two voices ('V', the voice of May's mother, emanating from the darkness upstage) and faint chimes divide *Footfalls* into three 'acts' and structure its gradually diminishing space, light and sound. Even in the context of this 'faint, though by no means invisible' (*CDW* 402) drama, its protagonist May does not amount to a character. Like many Beckett characters before her, she is not 'properly born', and has only a tenuous half-existence.[16] Even her name suggests potentiality rather than actuality, the subjunctive 'perhaps' that so fascinated Beckett from *Godot* onward, and no possessives are used to describe her minimal life. Like Beckett's other 'representative' M-figures, May walks, talks and hears voices; she cannot stop 'revolving it all' in her 'poor mind' (*CDW* 400). The slow, rhythmic dance of her steps is ghoulishly called by the invisible mother: 'But let us watch her move in silence [. . .] Watch how feat she wheels' (*CDW* 401). While the brief text of *Footfalls* is not spoken at the well-nigh incomprehensible rate of *Not I*, we only ever receive intimations of what 'it all' might be; every element of the play's exposition is rendered partial and fragmentary. As Anna McMullan notes, the lack of specific decor enables a simultaneous suggestion of an external, mimetic space, and/or an internal subjective one.[17] It is possible, therefore, that the 'deep sleep' from which May wakes V may suggest metaphorically the depths of memory or the grave, and thus that the scene is a memory being replayed in May's 'poor mind' in the present.

Footfalls' 'unborn' daughter May is yet another of the Beckett characters who are 'confined both within some restrictive space and within the limits of a text that revolves in their imagination'.[18] Like *Not I*'s Mouth and Beckett's female stage figures in general, May's struggle with words emphasizes her lack of identity; she cannot figure as a substantial presence within representation. Mary Bryden notes of the late plays that, while the primacy of voicing serves to emphasize the subject's quest for unity and identity, 'the uncertainty of its articulation and its frequent estrangement from stable speech-sources contribute to the perceived fragmentation of self'.[19] This is especially relevant to *Footfalls*, in which the capacity of the human voice to guarantee presence is fatally compromised by the distancing and dislocating device of the maternal echo, which undermines the notion of an origin as foundation of identity or authority.

Amidst the extreme indeterminacy of stage space and *mise-en-scène*, the initially apparently unambiguous relations of mother and daughter become blurred. While Voice, if taken as mother, is of course *literally* May's creator, she also seems to author May within language, playing both mother and daughter roles within the embedded dialogue in her narrative:

> May: Not enough. The mother: What do you mean, May, not enough, what can you possibly mean, May, not enough? May: I mean, Mother, that I must hear the feet, however faint they fall. The mother: The motion alone is not enough? May: No, Mother [...] (*CDW* 401)

May, on the other hand, herself attempts to take on the role of mother-author by creating an anagrammatic alter ego Amy and *her* mother, Mrs Winter, and also mirrors Voice's authorship by similarly playing both roles within her narrative. She 'voices', thus, both Amy, the daughter of this strange 'sequel' – 'a most strange girl, though scarcely a girl any more ... [*Brokenly*] ... dreadfully un- ...' (*CDW* 402) – and the mother who asks whether she has observed 'anything ... strange at Evensong' (*CDW* 403). The relationship between May and her ontologically ambiguous double (who denies her own attendance at Evensong, despite her apparent *bodily* presence) evokes the ambiguity of the identity and difference between May and Voice, and between May as we see her onstage and May as she appears in Voice's monologue.

The initial dialogue between May and Voice diverges into a chorus of polyphonic echoes that cause a certain leakage between the various relationships, sculpted minimally around hinted-at stories of marginality and ghostliness, like the 'tangle of tatters' (*CDW* 402). May's pacing is paralleled by her creation Amy's, and the mother–daughter dialogues-within-monologues form a paradoxically confusing symmetry. For the audience, the inevitable comparison arises between the faint but whole pacing body onstage, with its compulsive movement and pose of almost Cartesian self-absorption, and the multiple reflections and echoes of the several mother–daughter relationships represented in the spoken text. As a result, the fading ghost of the unitary self, authority and origin is dispersed by a preoccupation with echoes and a querying of the voice-as-presence. Within the four increasingly minimalist scenes of monologue, ritualized mother–daughter dialogue and compulsive, rhythmic pacing, various binaries – presence and absence, self and other, mother and daughter, author and authored – initially presented as polarities, are progressively undermined amid repeating cycles of diminution and loss.

Rockaby continues Beckett's preoccupation with the blurring of mother–daughter roles, and grafts it to the form of monological duet he evolved in *Krapp's Last Tape*, though without the onstage recording technology. A woman sits in a rocking chair, rocking to the tempo of memory as her recorded voice hypnotically repeats the brief elegiac phrases that encapsulate her life and its contracting spiral of desires. Enoch Brater suggests a parallel with W. B. Yeats's poem 'The Cold Heaven', as, like its speaker, W trembles and rocks 'to and fro, riddled with light';[20] in *Rockaby*, however, as the stage lights darken and the head slowly falls, no soul claps hands and sings. Instead, there is a slow fade-out, self-renouncing and hypnotic. Beckett told the producer of the 1981 Buffalo premiere, Daniel Labeille, that *Rockaby* was, above all, a lullaby, albeit one that rocks its speaker into oblivion.[21] (The title of the subsequent

French version, *Berceuse*, means both lullaby and rocking chair, while the English title recalls the sinister nursery rhyme in which the baby's cradle falls from a treetop, bringing together images of birth and death.)

Rockaby has four miniature 'acts', each depicting a progressive stage of W's quest. Each begins with a '*long pause*', then the 'live' voice getting the recorded one going, by demanding 'more' a little more softly each time, childlike, as though the taped voice is nourishment. Like Krapp, W interacts with her taped self, not only listening along with us to her own inner voice, but summoning it to start up again and joining with it to recite in a series of highly patterned voiceovers. *Rockaby*'s limited lexicon is printed not as prose dialogue but as a poem whose words move 'to and fro', 'high and low', to imitate the rocking chair, with pronouncedly hard phonemes matching the back-and-forth rhythms of the chair's rocking, and each line of printed text coinciding with each rock. 'All sides' of this verbal unit move back and forth: lines are rotated, made to formulate new permutations or allegiances with other words, then recombined in a new synthesis before reassuming the original shape in which we first encounter them:

> till in the end
> the day came
> close of a long day
> when she said
> to herself
> whom else
> time she stopped
> *time she stopped*
> going to and fro
> all eyes all sides high and low
> for another
> another like herself
> a little like

(*CDW* 435)

No image or situation is static, but is instead non-chronological, repetitious, spiralling, cumulative and fluid.

The compressed and oddly tender plot evokes the steps of a retreat from a failed search for 'another' towards death and fusion with the mother. The narrative first recounts an active search – 'All eyes | all sides' for 'Another creature like herself | A little like' – then a retreat to an upstairs window 'Facing other windows' and a familiar, but more static search 'For another | Another like herself | A little like | Another living soul' (*CDW* 435) watching and waiting at another window. When an even more muted search by her 'Famished eyes' for 'One blind up | No more | Never mind a face' (*CDW* 439) comes to nothing, W retreats 'Down the steep stair' to the 'Mother rocker', where her mother also rocked herself to death. As a death-dealing lullaby, the rhythmic speaking of the text becomes a rite of passage and transformation – from loss to (equivocal) comfort, from life to death and from incantatory speech to silence. As the motion of the chair falters to a halt at the play's end, along with the memory that moved it, the restless motion of desire – to and fro between self and other, seeker and sought – is also laid to rest.

A PIECE OF MONOLOGUE, OHIO IMPROMPTU AND *CATASTROPHE*

All three of these plays are highly and fruitfully self-conscious works, written by a playwright interested in revisiting familiar tropes, and reworking or recombining them. In some cases – specifically *Ohio Impromptu* – this is with an eye to an informed audience, familiar with the Beckett œuvre. In *A Piece of Monologue* and *Ohio Impromptu* Beckett turns his attention to how far language can go in sustaining tension on a bare and darkened set. Overturning Aristotelian ideas of heroic action, the monologue effectively becomes the dramatic action. *A Piece of Monologue* was first staged by La MaMa Theatre Club in New York in 1980, with David Warrilow as Speaker. The play presents a starkly immobile stage image: a dimly-lit figure of a white-haired old man, in white gown and socks, standing 'well off centre downstage' by an oil lamp, with the foot of a pallet dimly visible in the surrounding dark (*CDW* 425). His repetitive 'piece of monologue' describes a nocturnal routine that follows a strictly patterned ritual, lighting his oil lamp, gazing through the window at the 'black vast', gazing at the 'pin-

77

pocked' wall where once hung the photographs of those he cannot quite bring himself to call his 'ghost loved ones' (*CDW* 425). Speaker does not act out the nightly ritual; ritual speaking has replaced ritual doing. It is Beckett's language that takes centre stage in this monodrama; the figure who stands on stage is simply the necessary teller language needs to be spoken onstage, an only residually human mechanism for delivering the lines, in the sense that *Endgame*'s Hamm and Clov are kept on stage by 'the dialogue'. Speaker in *A Piece of Monologue* stands 'stock still [. . .] lip lipping lip' (*CDW* 428), the mere occasion for his speech. Character has been upstaged by discourse,[22] which is, in its turn, deadeningly second-hand. Many of the play's key terms, phrases and tropes – what the text dubs 'rip words' (*CDW* 429), evoking death ('R.I.P') as well as the violent emotions of memory – are familiar from frequent previous use in Beckett's writing, verbal remnants here reconvened and permuted into a mutedly and ambiguously 'new' stage text, as in *Rockaby*.

The title's 'piece' plays with the French *pièce* or play, suggesting 'a play on monologue', and the play certainly evokes a kind of muted anti- (or post-)*Hamlet*, with its '*skull-sized white globe*' (*CDW* 425), funerals of loved ones evoked with hallucinatory clarity, its bleak meditations on mortality, and its relentless peering 'beyond that black veil' (*CDW* 429). Characteristically, the economy of this confrontation with loss and renunciation is ferocious in its compression. In this play 'words are few' and 'dying too' (*CDW* 425). Speaker's monologue shrinks and attenuates Pozzo's 'They give birth astride of a grave' (*CDW* 83). In *A Piece of Monologue*, 'birth was the death of him', with cradle and grave conflated, the 'first totters' from 'mammy to nanny' seen as deathward bound, and movement through the 'two and a half billion seconds' of life as a brief progress 'from funeral to funeral' (*CDW* 425). The lamp-lighting ceremony, one critic suggests, offers a not-so-oblique metaphor for the sudden illumination offered by the playwright's continuing invention of stage dialogue, forever threatened by extinction but always on the alert for a last-minute reprieve.[23] Three funerals parallel the three lamp-lighting rituals, described with increasing economy. The two rituals – the lamp lighting and the funeral – have their onstage counterparts, the vertical lamp and the horizontal bed partly seen. 'Words are few' in this monologue, but, between the first 'birth' and the last 'gone', Beckett encapsulates the pattern for a universal biography, some fragments shored against universal ruins.

Beckett wrote *Ohio Impromptu* for an international symposium devoted to his work at Ohio State University in 1981. It is perhaps a rather knowing play, written for an audience of Beckett scholars, stirring evocations of Beckett reading to a blind Joyce; the 'Isle of Swans' (*CDW* 446) in Reader's narrative is where Beckett and Joyce walked together, the 'Latin Quarter hat' (*CDW* 446) is from the first episode of *Ulysses*, and the play's scenario evokes the popular myth that Beckett acted as Joyce's secretary on what would become *Finnegans Wake*. Moreover, the theatrical term 'impromptu' links the play to a theatrical tradition of impromptus such as Molière's *Impromptu de Versailles* and Ionesco's *Impromptu de l'Alma*, a playfully self-reflexive tradition that, according to Pierre Astier, deals 'with problems of play-acting or play-writing through the acting or writing of a play that turns out to be the very one performed before our eyes'.[24] The title, while amusingly inaccurate in suggesting extemporaneous composition, nonetheless announces the play's concern with the processes of creation, and the artistic practice of its author, as well as with the staging of the processes of autobiography: the self as creator of fictional alter egos or *Doppelgänger*. In a move typical of Beckett's late plays, a juxtaposition of narrative and visual image sets up an ambiguous dialogue, with each commenting upon the other, as the audience continually revises its view of the scenic image in the light of the text.

In contrast to many of the preceding solo plays, *Ohio Impromptu* presents a formally complete scenario of two white-haired male figures, as *'alike in appearance as possible'*, sitting at right angles to each other at a table. One reads a 'sad tale a last time told' (*CDW* 448) from a bound volume; one listens. When Listener knocks, Reader responds by pausing, doubling back and repeating the phrase he has just uttered, before continuing his narrative of a 'loved one' lost and subsequently regained, a grieving man and his nocturnal lector. His tale in fact, roughly, though not exactly, corresponds with the scene we see on stage before us, and appears to be the narrative or autobiography of the Listener who, by tapping on the table top, responds to it. The two figures, differentiated only by their function, mirror, but also confront each other, so that, even before a word of the text is spoken, the play has already set up, between the apparently binary oppositions of self and other, an ambiguous interplay of difference and identity, alterity and complementarity. Are Reader and Listener in fact the grieving man and the visiting reader of the narrative, and/or aspects of a schismatic self? What is the relationship between narration and presented scene? The stable stage image of two figures is muddied and complicated by the mass of coalescing and shifting relations between voice and listener, perceived and perceiver (that perennial Beckett theme), self-creating and self-created, being and telling, which the play spins across the confrontation of Reader and Listener. The scenic image can be read as a materialization of the processes of self-creation represented by the fictional or autobiographical text: the creator creates himself through the narrative and is created by it – the self being as much a retrospective fiction as the fictional self – in a 'process of scissiparity or schizogenesis' presented on stage.[25] *Ohio Impromptu* offers the possibility of being simultaneously autobiography, a kind of ur-fiction, and a metaphor for its own creation.

Sharing the self-consciousness of *Ohio Impromptu*, *Catastrophe* focuses on the power politics of making an arresting theatre image. Along with *What Where*, Beckett's last stage play, written in 1983, it returns to and develops Beckett's long-term preoccupation with questions of representation, authority and power. Composed originally in French, *Catastrophe* was dedicated to Vaclav Havel, and opened at the Avignon Festival in July 1982, as Beckett's contribution to a day of protest against the Czech dissident's incarceration.[26] Even without the dedication to Havel, the play confronts an audience with a disturbing vision of theatre as tyranny, somewhat akin to *Not I*. Gone are the tender, death-dealing rituals of the plays that immediately precede it. Instead, we encounter, with uncharacteristic naturalism, a bombastic and arrogant Director and his female assistant arranging a mute male 'Protagonist' on a pedestal,

apparently in rehearsal for a theatrical tableau that bears a
remarkable resemblance to Beckett's late theatrical style.

The Protagonist – ironically named, as he initiates no action
until his mute revolt at the very end of the play – is a version
of *Waiting for Godot*'s Lucky, hunched forlornly on a plinth and
subjected to objectification and humiliation, as tyrannical
Director and toadying Assistant vie with one another to control
the stage space and the figure suffering before them on the
block. Their interaction is a satiric parable of the making of a
theatre image, sometimes a blatant parody of it, as Beckett
self-consciously explores the ethics of a central paradox of his
theatre: the use of impersonal discipline, objectivity and
technology to make of human suffering a stage spectacle.

Some commentators have expressed surprise at the overtly
political commitment of the play. Initially performed at an
activist event, the play is, on the surface, more *engagé* than
anything else Beckett wrote. However, it only crystallizes the
muted and partial political allegories of earlier Beckett writings
– from interpretations of *Waiting for Godot* as stage metaphor
for post-Holocaust Europe and *Endgame* as post-nuclear
drama, to the more diffuse and interiorized typology of
oppression in Beckett's later work, whether the interrogating
spotlight in *Play* or the tin-opener torture into speech of the
crawlers of *How It Is*. Yet *Catastrophe*'s energy cannot be
contained by anything as neat as a denunciation of oppressive
regimes, and, in its preoccupation with power in its relation to
representation, it has implications that extend far beyond any
specific political context. While the play certainly evokes, in its
silent and subjected Protagonist, whose gagging is canvassed
by the Assistant, the predicament of the artist in an authoritarian regime, it also exposes the problematic nature of representation itself, as the mechanism of spectacle inevitably colludes
with the forces of authority and subjection. At the play's end,
dress-rehearsal becomes performance, with the surreal intrusion of the play audience's thunderous applause. Here, having
been subjected to the gaze of others throughout the play, the
Protagonist's raising of his head and return of the audience's
gaze suggest defiance and hopelessness as well as evoking the
Aristotelian responses of pity and fear, from both faltering play
audience and 'real' audience. His one autonomous gesture

81

subverts the pathetic little drama prepared for him by exposing and deflecting the gaze of power.

The major achievement of the 'dramaticules' is their attainment of a new kind of drama. In challenging many of theatre's basic conventions, they offer a characteristic counterpoint of verbal language and scenic detail. Generically complex, often presenting minimal and tattered narratives in a language strongly marked by rhythms and overwhelmed by intensified and polyvalent images, the late plays offer what Martin Esslin has influentially described as 'poetical metaphor concretised into a picture'.[27]

5

'Fancy dead': The Post-Trilogy Prose

Having largely exhausted the traditional resources of the novel, Beckett began, in the wake of the trilogy, to have recourse to what, along with drama, was to prove the most resilient and flexible genre in his career: shorter prose experiments. Rid of the weight of the novel, the late prose constitutes a body of writing of rigorously diminished expectations, 'texts for nothing', a renewed push towards what he had called in 1937, in full modernist demolition drive, 'the literature of the unword' (D. 173). In these short texts, for which Beckett coined a variety of apparently dismissive names – *Residua*, *From an Abandoned Work*, *Fizzles* – the self-negation of language, which began in the trilogy, seems capable of persevering indefinitely. The shorter prose texts finger obsessively the fundamental Beckettian obsession with the deconstruction of the writing process. As early as his 1931 study of *Proust*, Beckett asserted that the 'artistic tendency is not expansive, but a contraction' (*PTD* 47), and this is certainly at issue throughout the post-trilogy prose, in which radical experimentation and severe compression occur side by side, producing writing that is minimalist in scope, but not in ambition.

While the minimalism of the theatre pieces of the 1970s and 1980s is often lyrical, that of the late prose is the far harsher affair of a writer relishing complete control of his few remaining materials, undisturbed by the unpredictable human elements of actors, director, spectators. These are texts treated as experimental spaces in which their author is answerable to no one as he conducts what seems at times, so disdainful is it of the needs or expectations of any putative readership, to be a writing of pure research, intended for no audience. His experiments are largely deconstructive, concerned with the further negation of the classical forms of fictional narrative, and with the destroying of fiction through fiction. Some of the prose pieces (*All Strange Away*, some of the *Fizzles*) are unfinished fragments; others return again and again to a body within a circumscribed environment as a form of denuded still life. Yet others (*Enough, From an Abandoned Work*) approach conventional narrative in ways that seem weirdly expansive compared to the desiccated monochromatic minimalism of other late prose pieces. While the paralysing final words of *The Unnamable* seemed at the time to represent an impasse, Beckett's writings are nevertheless compelled to go on unsaying themselves again and again in increasingly impoverished ways.

TEXTS FOR NOTHING

The thirteen *Texts for Nothing*, which Beckett originally wrote in French in 1950–1, have frequently been seen as a mere succession of misfires, signalling the end of Beckett's great creative period of 1946–50, as an afterthought or faint residual stuttering from the impulse that created *The Unnamable*. Beckett himself encouraged this dismissive attitude by his own references to the *Texts* as expressing 'the failure to implement the last words of *The Unnamable*: "I can't go on, I'll go on".'[1] It seems undeniable that, the extreme creativity of the 'siege in the room' beginning to flag, Beckett returned to short fiction in his struggle to 'go on'. The result was thirteen fragmentary texts grouped together under a title adapted from the musician's phrase denoting a bar's rest, *mesure pour rien* in the original French; the suggestion is one of struggle, futility and encroaching silence. Similarities to the final trilogy novel are certainly not hard to find. The opening of the first of the texts returns us to the same uncertain situation as the end of *The Unnamable* – a space where recognizable external reality and discrete literary characters have given place to a naked voice, strangely disembodied, sourceless and driven to speak, des-

84

pairingly persistent in its failure to stop saying: 'Suddenly, no, at long last, I couldn't any more. I couldn't go on' (*CSP* 100). Gone, however, is the sense of narrative trajectory and increasingly frenetic and panicky crescendo that bound the still-linear, still-novelistic *The Unnamable* together, and moved it towards its inconclusive conclusion: 'I can't go on, I must go on, I'll go on.'

In *Texts for Nothing*, the reader encounters only splinters of time and place, the mere shards of what are no longer in any sense 'completed' tales, and muted narrative squibs suggesting voyages that never go anywhere: 'no need of a story, a story is not compulsory, just a life, that's the mistake I made, one of the mistakes, to have wanted a story for myself, whereas life alone is enough' (*CSP* 116). 'Life' here does not mean 'a life' in the sense of a coherent story or character, as these are concepts that *Texts for Nothing* has abandoned, but a residual 'life' in the sense of the minimal vital signs of the Beckett predicament, the necessity to 'go on' still flickering away amidst the plethora of disembodied voices and the shards of what might have been stories. The network of often arch allusions to the eighteenth-century 'Graveyard' school of poets – Young's celebrated *Night Thoughts*, with its language of crepuscular liminality and doomy rhetoric and Gray's 'Elegy in a Country Churchyard', with its night birds, obsession with the ephemeral, elegiac metre and tonal palette in shades of dimness – seem to stand behind many of the twilight passages throughout the *Texts*, as H. Porter Abbott points out.[2] In fact, Beckett, in referring to the Romantic tradition, as he does again in *Imagination Dead Imagine* (1965), marks his apartness from anachronistic Romantic self-confidence and expansiveness. In Beckett's hands the looseness and fragmentariness of the *Texts*, far from expressing confidence in the synthesizing powers of the individual mind, laments an inability to connect and cohere.

It is not possible to offer plot summaries of the *Texts for Nothing*, as, both at the level of narrative 'event' and at the micro-level of the individual sentence, new developments or words are rejected as unsuitable as soon as said, though their continued presence on the page undermines what succeeds the cancelled material. Narrative squibs are damped down as soon as they take fire. Positive assertions are countered or modified with negatives coming close on their heels. The result is what one critic dubs a 'legible palimpsest',[3] a laying-bare of the visibly tormented processes of composition. *Texts for Nothing* constitutes an exposure of narrative, presenting us throughout with a despairingly garrulous first-person speaker who continually demonstrates its assorted inadequacies as narrator. Uncertainty runs riot throughout the texts. In Text I, the speaking voice hears another voice, perhaps more than one, and addresses a recalcitrant body and head as though they were stage props, rather like the disembodied heads or bodily fragments of the late drama: 'I say to the body, Up with you now, and I can feel it struggling, like an old hack foundered in the street' (*CSP* 100). Through the speaking of this voice, evanescent scenes and characters – apparently coming from 'above', 'where the living find their ways' (*CSP* 105) – take shape briefly: in Text I the familiar Beckett tramp, indigent, transient, prostrate in boggy terrain, in Text II brief vignettes about the bag lady Mother Calvet, 'her dog and her skeletal baby buggy' and Mr Joly the one-legged bell ringer, while Text III, the longest, deploys a nanny named Bibby and a 'crony' named Vincent. The end of Text III, however, undermines even these rudimentary flexings of the weakening narrative impulse, with the interruption of a shockingly naked first-person narrator: 'I'm here, that's all I know, and that it's still not me, it's of that the best has to be made. There is no flesh anywhere, nor any way to die' (*CSP* 113). The first-person narrator, in its placeless indeterminate 'here', can never be identified with any of its creatures, become sufficiently embodied into flesh or narrative to find death. The concluding texts, from Text X's opening 'Give up' onward, accomplish additional surrenders and relinquishments from this already impoverished position. Texts X, XII and XIII manage entirely without recourse to 'story', making the reader look back on the first three texts, which on first reading seemed so barren, appear in comparison positively lavish in their attention to detail.

The role of the *Texts for Nothing* is chiefly important in terms of genre, as it marks Beckett's adoption or invention of the 'text', which would figure increasingly in his œuvre after this time. A 'short work with no real subject but its own queer cohesion', as Hugh Kenner defines it, it becomes a recurrent and flexible mode in Beckett's hands.[4] In this sense, then, the

Texts are a new departure, prefiguring his evisceration of the short story, much as the trilogy, and later *How It Is*, do for the novel form. Rather than being discarded segments or impulses cobbled together out of the afterbirth of *The Unnamable*, *Texts for Nothing* renovates Beckett's œuvre by entirely discarding both the quest and the linear narrative as a whole in favour of this gapped, discontinuous and non-linear mode of writing.

HOW IT IS

The next major prose work after the *Texts for Nothing*, Beckett's grotesque anti-epic *How It Is*, was written almost a decade later, and was first published in French in 1961. It was entitled in French *Comment c'est* ('how it is', 'how things are'), and the critics immediately noticed in the uncharacteristically confident declaration of the title a network of homophonic puns – *commencez* ('begin'), *commencer* ('to begin') and other forms of the same verb. This was interpreted by some critics as a declaration that Beckett's creative powers in prose had been reborn after long silence. The same critics were frustrated then to encounter a novel-length work with an appalling diagrammatic simplicity that would become familiar in the later prose, entirely without narrative suspense. In the world of this text, 'how it is' constitutes the doings of a minimal creature crawling forward through a subterranean world of mud, with his few belongings clutched to him in a coal sack, his torment of another, similar, creature, and his torture in turn at the hands of a third creature. The torture constitutes a cruelly elaborate semiotic system, the victim in each case coerced into responding to a 'table of basic stimuli' administered by the right hand of the tormentor as follows: 'one sing nails in armpit | two speak blade in arse three stop thump on | skull four louder pestle on kidney' (*HII* 69), and also to questions scratched with fingernails on his back. In response to the tormentor's commands to tell about his life 'ABOVE [...] IN THE LIGHT' (*HII* 77), the victim recites scraps of narrative of 'that life then said to have been his invented remembered a little of each no knowing' (*HII* 88). This pattern is then hypothesized by the speaker as a mere link in a chain of alternate suffering and torment that extends around the globe, each creature taking his turn as victim and tormenter.

How It Is is Beckett's sardonic rewriting of the epic, the prestigious literary form that traditionally tells the reader 'how it is' in the sense of explicating the world and its origins. For instance, in Christian epic, this extends to justifying apparently capricious divine deeds to mankind, as in *Paradise Lost*, or showing how divine justice allots a post-mortem punishment to fit the crime, as in Beckett's revered *Divine Comedy*. *How It Is* contains a tapestry of muted allusions to the epic tradition. The relentless circularity of the world of the text, the evocation of endless torment according to a certain notion of 'justice', the almost-quotation 'abandon hope', all suggest Dante's *Inferno*, while it has been suggested that the continual references to 'the life above in the light before I fell' (*HII* 86) recall Satan in *Paradise Lost*. However, far from offering an *hommage* to traditional epic, Beckett's appallingly even-handed reign of terror, and its world of solitude, mud and suffering, operate according to a bleakly mathematical notion of justice, with each creature taking its turn in the roles of victim and tormentor. The only 'injustice' recognized by Beckett's epic bard is the potential for a fault in the system to result in a tormentor left victimless, and a victim left without his tormentor.

Working out the symmetry of this universal order is the challenge of Beckett's bard, with the final section of *How It Is* becoming a curiously mathematical affair, in which the increasingly anguished speaker tries and fails to work out in numerical terms the entirety of the system he has been elaborating in terms of a few individuals. He proclaims in the final pages that his construction is hopelessly flawed, and packs away the epic tradition. With the failure of authorship and poetic authority, the epic mode, traditionally the most overweening and authoritative of all modes, is made to fail. The anointed, chosen, inspired, muse-evoking epic poet, selected by a higher power to convey an absolute truth, in Beckett's hands becomes a faulty, feeble mathematician who, far from sending his song soaring Milton-like, is miserably aware of the imperfect and constructed nature of his narrative.

Far from endorsing the authoritative and divinely inspired language of epic, *How It Is* offers the reader an utterly 'fallen', pun-laden world of linguistic 'ooze'. Entirely without punctuation, except for the white spaces of page between its brief 'strophes', it consists entirely of short paragraph-length blurts of words. It is impossible to skim the text for some easily identifiable 'content'; reading is simultaneously fast-forwarded into a jerky floundering onward into unpunctuated, pun-laden, 'oozing' language, and, paradoxically, also slowed down into a sluggish groping forward into a kind of textual mud, as the language enacts the minimal 'story' of *How It Is*, which is 'ill-murmured ill-heard ill-recorded my whole life a gibberish garbled sixfold' (*HII* 146). If this were not enough, the voice we encounter in *How It Is* is ambiguous in source. The very first paragraph announces the entire work as an act of quotation: 'how it was I quote before Pim with Pim after Pim how it is three parts I say it as I hear it' (*HII* 7). The controlling fiction of *How It Is*, then, is that the narrator's life is being dictated to him from the outside, and, as that narrative act contains references to a source dictating to it, we are left with the possibility that there is an infinite regression of sources, an unlocatable speech. The narrator seems less an individual, a person with a history, than a kind of stopping point for voices, a junction of extorted speech acts, a collection depot for words whose source remains uncertain. (This bewildering plurality of the speaking subject is, of course, a central theme and technique in the trilogy and *Texts for Nothing*, as well as being dramatized in *Krapp's Last Tape*.) One could read the quotational hall of mirrors of *How It Is* – a speaker quoting the words of a speaker who is quoting the words of a speaker who is quoting, and so on ad infinitum – as picking up its quotational device from the closing lines of the last of the *Texts for Nothing*: 'as soon now, when all will be ended, all said, it murmurs' (*CSP* 154). Travestying the traditional epic mode, *How It Is* offers instead a hopelessly 'fallen' epic for the second half of the twentieth century.

THE LOST ONES

The Lost Ones was substantially written in French as *Le Dépeupleur* in 1966, but lay incomplete and abandoned until 1970, before publication in French in 1971, followed by English in 1972. One of the more substantial pieces of the late prose – fifty-seven pages in its original format – *The Lost Ones* partakes of the anti-epic vision of *How It Is*. The text offers a detailed, deadpan description of a confined and miniature world of sterile desolation, in which 200-odd 'lost bodies' are described at rest and in motion, acting according to their own rules and conventions, suffering, and punishing infractions. Some, referred to by the text's scrupulously detached narrator as 'amateurs of myth', believe in the existence 'from time immemorial' of 'a way out' of their incarceration, although disagreeing as to this hypothetical exit's location, while others, still roaming, have lapsed from 'that old belief' (*CSP* 206). Over fifteen unnumbered subsections, the location of the search – a 'flattened cylinder fifty metres round and eighteen high for the sake of harmony'[5] – is analysed, the customs governing the behaviour of its inhabitants are minutely classified and the habits of the various factions described.

The cylinder's active inhabitants mill about the floor of the cylinder or file Indian-fashion along the walls, waiting in lines to take turns in climbing the fifteen ramshackle ladders, which offer a panorama of the crowd from above, or allow access to the maze of niches and tunnels in the cylinder's walls, 'disposed quincuncially for the sake of harmony'. Others, the zombie-like ranks of the ex-searchers, known as the 'vanquished' (*CSP* 210), no longer search. Equally fulsome accounts are offered of ladder etiquette, the curiously infernal atmospheric conditions that prevail, and its consequences for the shrivelled 'mucous membrane' of the inhabitants, as well as obsessive mathematical calculations of every detail – the length of the ladders, the surface area of the cylinder, and so on. However, all activity in the cylinder is 'issueless'; not only is the goal of the search elusive, but the cylinder itself is running down into entropy, according to which 'in the beginning then unthinkable as the end all roamed without respite' (*CSP* 212–13). The fifteenth and final segment of the text does, however, think this 'unthinkable' end, in which only a 'last body of all is searching still', until he at last 'finds his place and pose whereupon dark descends and at the same instant the temperature comes to rest not far from the freezing point' (*CSP* 223). The narrative ends with all life in the cylinder apparently extinguished.

A network of references to 'sulphur' and 'pandemonium' (*CSP* 209), and references to the non-searching inhabitants of the cylinder sitting like Belacqua in the lee of the wall 'in the attitude which wrung from Dante one of his rare wan smiles' (*CSP* 205), suggest that, like *How It Is*, *The Lost Ones* also leans consciously against the epic tradition. This latest epic bard, however, writes in a scrupulously bland manner likened by one critic to 'a report by a Civil Service Commission enquiring into the conditions in Purgatory'[6] and, rather more aptly, by another to the 'description of an exotic tribe by a diligent ethnographer given at times to quaint orotundities of style and occasional patronizing compliments for the cylinder's system's adequacy in meeting the needs of its citizens'.[7] This travesty of epic justifies the goings-on in its miniature world via unconvincing banalities, which become sinister through their failure to engage with the suffering of this world's denizens: 'So all is for the best' (*CSP* 216). The apparently bland surface of its prose is continually being unsettled, and its blandishments undermined, by paradox ('Paradoxically, the sedentary are those whose acts of violence most disrupt the cylinder's quiet' (*CSP* 205)), arbitrariness (the dimensions of the cylinder appear to have been chosen 'for the sake of harmony' (*CSP* 202)), oxymoron ('making unmakeable love' (*CSP* 214)), sudden wanings of interest ('so much for a first apercu of the abode' (*CSP* 204)), and naked confessions of ignorance on the part of this purportedly omniscient narrator ('all has never been told and never shall be' (*CSP* 219)). If *The Lost Ones* is in fact Beckett's homage to Dante, a succinct *Inferno* for the late twentieth century, it is one narrated by an unconvinced and incapacitated epic bard, whose fragile envisioned 'abode' lasts only as long as 'this notion is maintained' (*CSP* 223). In both *How It Is* and *The Lost Ones*, then, the epic urge is soured and miniaturized, and ravaged by the forms of uncertainty and ignorance traditional epic suppresses.

RESIDUA[8]

With the possible exception of the 8,000-word *The Lost Ones*, in the geometric world beyond *How It Is*, Beckett's minimalism becomes far more harshly evident, as does the fact that the late prose is marked – indeed, is characterized – by its own strategies of reduction and compression. There are clear parallels with the miniaturization, generic blurring and dog-gedly anti-mimetic stance of the late dramaticules. Here genre is under equal stress, to the extent that the editor of Beckett's *Collected Shorter Prose* has to provide copious annotations on the generic roaming of late texts such as *From an Abandoned Work*, now settled in the prose canon, but which was initially published as a theatre piece by Faber in *Breath and Other Shorts* (1972), and the tiny 'neither', which has been published at various times with or without line breaks suggestive of poetry. (It was at one point to have been included in Beckett's *Collected Poems*, rather than any prose collections.[9]) Though both are now generally classed as prose works, they remain sympto-matic of the radical generic bleeding that occurs in the late prose, and its pronounced tendency to inhabit, often disturb-ingly, the margins between prose and poetry or performance, and – in a late period studded with titles such as *Fizzles*, *Residua* and *From an Abandoned Work* – completion and incompletion.

Any kind of chronology becomes progressively more diffi-cult to establish, as the late prose texts become increasingly interconnected and self-referential, in part because of the jerky process of abandonment and 'unabandonment' by which Beckett's prose writing moved in its late phase, with fragments of longer, temporarily or permanently abandoned works often being separately published. For instance, the French fragment 'L'Image' (published in the journal *X*, 1959) and the English fragment 'From an Unabandoned Work' (*Evergreen Review*, 1960) were both segments of *How It Is*, released for publication when it seemed unlikely *How It Is* would be completed. Similarly, the French *Bing*, translated into English as *Ping*, was described by Beckett as 'the result or miniaturization of *Le Dépeupleur* [*The Lost Ones*] abandoned because of its intractable complexities'.[10] Despite the fact that *The Lost Ones* was eventu-ally completed, having been 'abandoned' between 1966 and 1970, *Ping* – and its enigmatic sibling text *Lessness* – retain their status as texts in their own right. Other constellations of fragments cluster around more sustained works – *Heard in the*

Dark 1 and *2* are early versions of the novel *Company* (1980) –
while still other texts appear literally to generate each other via
repetition. *Imagination Dead Imagine*, for instance, evolves out
of *All Strange Away*, the title of the latter becoming the opening
lines of the former. Thus, over this period, Beckett's work
evolves a kind of poetics of incompletion, making of impasse
an opportunity for 'going on', if not actual aesthetic triumph.

If the prose of the trilogy continually exhorted itself to 'go
on', the late prose circles itself guardedly and revisits itself in
profoundly disconcerting ways. *Imagination Dead Imagine*, as
well as being a textual descendant of *All Strange Away*, in its
final depiction of 'that white speck lost in whiteness' (*CSP* 185)
provides the starting point for the situation of *Ping*, which
transposes that image into 'All known all white bare white
body' (*CSP* 193). In a curious restatement of the 'form and
content' debate the young Beckett carried on in his criticism, it
is as though the superficial content of these interrelated works
is very much a given, but the subject of the work is the text
itself, or rather how to keep rewriting that text. Recurrent
images are easily discerned in these works, in which apparently living bodies are treated as still lives.

In *Ping*, a little body is enclosed in a white cube, its blue eyes
simultaneously the only sign of colour and the only sign of life
(a sign that seems to be associated with the abrupt intrusion
into the prose of the word 'ping'). In *Lessness*, the governing
colour is now ash-grey, the skeletal scenario a tiny, rigid, grey
body in a landscape of grey ruins, grey sand and grey sky (*CSP*
197–201). *All Strange Away*, after accomplishing the impossible
in its opening words – imagining the death of the imagination
– follows up a wearily self-referential passage in which the
familiar trajectory of the typical Beckett vagrant is canvassed
and rejected, by opting to construct and measure a confined
world obeying elementary geometric rules. *Imagination Dead
Imagine* is a residual version of *All Strange Away*, concentrating
entirely on the rotunda of the last part of the previous text,
populated by two figures lying back to back. It is as if the
written has become solid, three-dimensional, and must be
assimilated from all sides, as though these texts have solidified
into what one critic has called a kind of 'frozen verbal
sculpture'.[11] In recirculating rudimentary material already

tried and tested – descriptions of ruins and illuminated rotunda, the body's postures – Beckett is acknowledging the obsessiveness of the imagination. The classic Beckettian opposition of observer and observed comes into being once again, in denuded scenarios where a single static image is 'ill seen' and consequently 'ill said', to borrow the title of a later prose work.

The creation of these patterns of fundamental sounds, in which words have simply become sparse, penurious objects in a vacuum, is, however, an arduous task. Beckett's late prose positions itself on the aporia first expressed in the *Three Dialogues*, balanced between the obligation to express and an equally powerful struggle against expression. The distrust of narrative evinced from the beginning of Beckett's career here becomes a set of strategic attempts to restrict literature to the bare bones of communication, relentlessly concrete and external, all 'fancy dead' (*CSP* 171). It is possible, as Andrew Renton argues, to see Beckett's later work as a 'constantly reiterated strategy against content', or an expression that occurs despite itself.[12] Certainly, in the late prose, we witness a series of bleak and tight-lipped attempts to abolish figurative language, to construct literary texts entirely without metaphor, texts that will literally defeat themselves.

S. E. Gontarski argues that Beckett is essentially adapting the aesthetic of architecture, Mies van der Rohe's 'less is more' and Adolf Loos's 'ornament is a crime', to prose, setting out to expunge ornament, strip inessentials and cultivate a language of ideally impoverished meanings and references.[13] *Ping* and *Lessness* work like prose poems, with an oddly congealed or frozen prose, a few descriptive elements shaken together into verbless, syntax-less sentences, and permuted and recombined, forcing the reader to scan similar, though not identical, phrases, for slight variations. This has led one critic to suggest a source for *Ping* in Beckett's experience of making his *Film* in New York in 1964, suggesting that a preoccupation with film would account for the emphasis on lighting, the absence of detail, as though in overexposure, and the lack of verbs: 'Each frame of a film is *so*, like a noun, and the action, normally specified by verbs, is an illusion generated by the frame's successiveness.'[14]

94

Certainly, the effect of the permutation of phrases is quite different from that of earlier works like *Watt*, where the effect was of compulsiveness, an attempt to exhaust possibility in the face of the inexplicable. Here the effect is more like a dance, or a highly ordered poetic form like the sestina, an austerely formal rearrangement of phrases strangely at odds with *Lessness*'s evocation of the aftermath of cataclysm and burned-out ruins. *Imagination Dead Imagine*, on the other hand, is intent on expunging all traces of evocative literary settings, evoked in terms that recall the Romantic imagination ('islands, waters, azure, verdure' (*CSP* 182)), and contemptuously and imperiously instructs the reader instead to envisage the ultimate in artistic impoverishment, the death of the imagination. Imagination being dead, the text contemplates the by now familiar rotunda and its male and female inhabitants, curled up foetus-like 'ashen or leaden or between the two' (*CSP* 183), plotting the precise positions of the immobile bodies by means of geometrical coordinates. The narrator records his minute observations with extreme precision, supplying letters to help us diagram the half-circles in which these creatures lie. His language yaws uneasily between the mathematical ('two diameters at right angles AB CD') and the allusive and poetic ('a ring as in the imagination the ring of bone') and is clearly under strain (*CSP* 182).

Palpably, these blank, stripped texts inevitably figure despite themselves. *Imagination Dead Imagine* has frequently been read as the last vestige of a dying imagination, 'itself a proof that the imagination is not yet dead: a fertilized stillborn egg, or an almost dead star lost in orbit'.[15] Or it is a terminal vision of a post-atomic world in which the remnants of humanity, a nuclear winter Adam and Eve, lie emphatically expelled from the 'verdure, azure' of Eden, unprotected from the unfriendly elements, yet still, barely, alive. Other critics have read an allusion to *King Lear* in the evocation of mirror and scant breath, and read Beckett's text as a reduced and soured version of Shakespeare's 'bare fork'd creature'. The *Residua* remain enigmatic in their stripped-down efforts to reduce the body to voiceless, static textual object, named only by geometric signifiers as though in an attempt to reduce being to a simple matter of mathematical formulae. Utterly iconoclastic, and rigidly penurious, this is a writing that appears to have been purged of all but its own relentless concreteness, but which, by the very nature of its compelling blankness, retains a potential suggestiveness.

NOHOW ON

Company (1980), and its successors, *Ill Seen Ill Said* (1981) and *Worstward Ho* (1983), are all of relatively substantial length, given the brevity of the works of the previous decade. In this, they seemed to announce a movement of more sustained writing after a decade of deadpan fragments and intricately self-defeating 'fizzles'. Published together in 1989 as *Nohow On*, and often referred to as Beckett's 'Second Trilogy', these three 'novels' flower out into a late richness of tone and form, after the astringent starkness of preceding years, despite retaining a degree of lexical impoverishment.

Company, in particular, was hailed as a strikingly intimate new departure, gravitating 'more openly toward the genre of autobiography than anything before it',[16] and, according to another critic, constituting a veritable 'backstage pass' or invitation into the author's mind.[17] Beckett's first biographer, Deirdre Bair, suggested that the publication of her biography in 1978 may have influenced its writing, and an influential reading of the text adapts this reasoning and sees *Company* as an emergency response to Bair's 'false narrative', purporting to be the story of Samuel Beckett's life.[18] Certainly the work's multiple retrospections constitute a virtual family reunion of old tropes, allusions and dramatis personae (Belacqua, greatcoats, larches, Dante, Milton) from Beckett's past, and some nakedly autobiographical sections (the 'loved trusted face' of a paternal figure resembling Bill Beckett (C. 18), the kamikaze climb to 'near the top of a great fir' (C. 21), the Wicklow mountains) combine to suggest a muted sense of self-conscious finale to a life's work.

Yet *Company* combats this impulse towards self-representation or self-recognition with an opposing movement towards chaos and uncertainty, as the text doubles and divides itself, dispersing the subjective 'I' among second- and third-person narratives, among a chain of narrators or 'devisers', devising stories for their muted ability to keep the speaker company. A work about Beckettian 'sociability', as Leo Bersani and Ulysse Dutoit have dubbed it,[19] *Company* begins as a purely formal exercise: 'A voice comes to one in the dark. Imagine' (*C*. 7). The next paragraph expands slightly on this: 'To one on his back in the dark a voice tells of a past. With occasional allusions to a present and more rarely to a future as for example, You will end as you now are' (*C*. 8). At the same time a motive is given for the imagining about to take place: 'And in another dark or in the same another devising it all for company' (*C*. 14). The 'company' of the title is the accumulation of self-generated constructions, in the forms of inventions and memories, that people the world of the writer's imagination, and the text posits the question of what kind of companionship these fragments can offer their creator, and their relation to him, their 'devised deviser'.

However, unlike previous works such as *The Unnamable*, *Texts for Nothing* and *Not I*, *Company* generates no sense of despair or self-alienated inauthenticity; although schismatic, chaotic and broken, it is fruitfully so. In its elaborate explora- tion of the divisions between the double narrators – the second-person narrative in highly autobiographical mode, the third-person mobile and disruptive – and thus of the narration, it focuses attention upon the processes of narrative itself, and in so doing reveals the splits, chasms and lacunae that exist in all narratives. *Company*, despite its air of approachability and affability, thereby aligns itself against closure, tidiness of form and unification of meaning. It is, in its way, as radical a rewriting of autobiography as *How It Is* or *The Lost Ones* of epic.

Ill Seen Ill Said likewise employs highly personal subject matter to formally innovative ends. A widespread and perva- sive reading of this fiction has it that the old woman – be she ghost, memory or fiction – who 'whitens afar' in the dark cabin and its surrounding 'zone of stones' is May Beckett, the detrimental effects of whose 'savage loving' on her son have become part of critical myth.[20] Certainly the relentless trembl- ing the text enacts thematically and syntactically – a landscape first drooping motionless, then shivering 'under the relentless eye [. . .] with the faintest shiver from its innermost', hair that alternates being 'rigidly horrent' (*ISIS* 18) with sudden move-ment, a narrative syntax alternately still and in motion under the motion of the watching eye – would seem appropriate to the Parkinson's Disease of which May Beckett died. Its symptoms of increasingly violent shaking interspersed with periods of total rigidity appear frequently in Beckett's later writing, as it became increasingly attentive to the multiple incapacities of the ill and ageing body, 'that scandal', as *Ill Seen Ill Said* dubs it (*ISIS* 19). There is also a terrible, possessive power in the words 'She shows herself only to her own. But she has no own. Yes yes she has. And who has her' (*ISIS* 6), which seem to indicate that the haunting is a kind of private possession of the rapacious eye and brain of the text by the lost woman, who is neither living nor dead, vacillating as she is on the cusp of what the text describes as the 'real and – how ill say its contrary? The counter-poison' (*ISIS* 18–19).

Confusion blurs the distinction between what is real and what not: 'If only she could be pure figment. Unalloyed. This old so dying woman. So dead' (*ISIS* 10–11). It is this distinctly Edgar Allan Poe-like quality of living death that *Ill Seen Ill Said* evokes most vividly, in its ghost-story scenario, faintly *fin de siècle* vocabulary, and its continual emphasis on trembling and looking. Its central event is the haunting of the rapacious widowed eye by the simultaneously living and dead figure of the black-clad old woman who 'comes and goes' – like the short lyric strophes of the text – 'all in black' to and fro from a tomb that may be her own. *Ill Seen Ill Said* constitutes a poetic evocation of those rituals by which both living and dead (always porous categories in this œuvre) within Beckett's writing endlessly and vainly strive to attain a definitive ending. Try as they may, Beckett's long-suffering protagonist and the ghostly 'she' whom he can never quite forget remain victims of 'Remembrance! When all worse there than when first ill seen' (*ISIS* 37).

In *Worstward Ho*, Beckett's last major prose work, another incompetent, barely living narrative stumbles into an expression of the desire to 'Know no more. See no more. Say no more' in order to savour 'That little much of void alone' (*WH* 18). The sardonically dour title, with its gamut of references to John Webster and Thomas Dekker's *Westward Hoe* (1607) and

Charles Kingsley's *Westward Ho!* (1855), withholds the expected panache of an exclamation mark after the usually jolly
'Ho', while 'westward' takes a bizarrely fruitful turn for the
worse. In this text, worse is better, the more 'ill said' the better,
because the closer to the ineffable end for which all Beckett's
long-suffering protagonists long. Fiction is being deployed to
destroy fiction by unsaying it through repetition. In fact, this
project is outlined more explicitly in *Worstward Ho* than in any
previous Beckett text – 'Try again. Fail again. Fail better' (*WH*
7) – as it becomes a synthesis of his desired 'literature of the
unword' (*D.* 173), with narrative itself structured as a series of
subtractions.

A minimal voice begins by exhorting itself to continue: 'On.
Say on' (*WH* 7). This unpromising beginning, as so often in
Beckett, gradually builds itself into not one but three minimal
stories: first a body that gathers to itself sufficient 'remains of
mind' (*WH* 9) to suffer; then a 'head sunk on crippled hands',
identified nonetheless as the 'germ of all' (*WH* 10); and finally,
and most elaborately, 'an old man and a child' who walk
together 'joined by held holding hands' (*WH* 13). *Worstward Ho*
goes on to hypothesize 'a place. Where none. Thenceless
thitherless there', though removing the possibility of movement attempts to exclude any suggestion of place, since place
can be defined only by movements towards or from. Yet
Worstward Ho generates an extended text from this refusal to
progress, and in its way becomes an eminently linear narrative
about precisely this impossibility. Narrative is generated by the
overt suppression of intent, the ghostly cast being set hesitant-
ly in motion, being 'worsened', each in turn, several times, the
voice returning to 'try worsen' (*WH* 23) as a means of getting
'somehow on' (*WH* 37). All the phantom dramatis personae are
eventually worsened out of existence, and the voice, its
materials for worsening gone, and the potential for going on
by worsening almost gone, concludes in impotence: 'Nohow
on' (*WH* 47). *Worstward Ho* reduces language to a 'most mere
minimum. Mere-most minimum' (*WH* 9), and uses this stubbornly residual vitality to (de)-construct a disquieting epiph-
any of 'missaying'.

Worstward Ho was not the final prose work Beckett wrote.
Other fragmentary texts followed during the 1980s, ending in

1988, the year before Beckett's death, with *Stirrings Still*, a brief tripartite work almost entirely composed of echoes and reiterations of his previous writing, especially the plays *Nacht und Träume* (published in 1984) and *Ohio Impromptu*, with their scenes of some form of devised figment of the self providing 'company' for a solitary protagonist. This mutedly poignant meditation on death brings to a conclusion the rigorous and compressed experiments of the late prose, its interrogation of the myth of representational adequacy and its distillation of a personal idiolect. What *Breath* does for theatre, taking it as close to nullity as a practising playwright could come, the post-trilogy prose does for the novel and short story, already subjected to deconstruction in Beckett's early fiction and the trilogy. A. Alvarez suggests that the late prose is Beckett's 'equivalent of the advanced metallurgy of space flight, a medium which is neutral, almost weightless, yet able to withstand enormous stress'.[21] Certainly, in its precise and desiccated minimalism, it moves beyond conveying a 'mocking attitude towards the word, through words' – to revert to the young Beckett's prescient modernist ambitions – and pushes closer to his cherished 'literature of the unword', or the 'savage economy of hieroglyphics' (D. 173, 28).

6

Screens and Sounds: Radio, Film and Television Drama

The austerity of much of Beckett's work for stage and page would appear to make him an unlikely match for the popular media of radio, film and television, with their association with mass entertainment, emphasis on commercial programming and fostering of audience passivity. In fact, Beckett's radio and television dramas, and his one foray into film, were frequently written in response to hints, if not outright commissions, by friends and trusted collaborators. Such suggestions led Beckett to experiment in media it seems unlikely he would otherwise have approached. Ultimately, these experiments elicited some of his most disquieting and original gestures towards the 'literature of the unword', as he dubbed it in 1937 (*D.* 173), from the radio play *All That Fall* (1957) to the final, wordless television plays *Nacht und Träume* and *Quad* (1984). Since these suggestions specified a medium, rather than a topic, Beckett tended to allow the new medium to generate its own subject, often resulting in a fascinated self-referential meditation on the nature of the novel medium for which he is writing.

Certainly, the so-called media plays have never had the impact of his stage plays – in part, it has been suggested, because of their relative lack of circulation. They have frequently remained largely unbroadcast after their premieres, publicly accessible only as a published script that, in the case of the wordless television play *Quad*, is merely an unevocative diagram of player movement.[1] However, Beckett's perpetual search for more concise distillations of expression, and desire to escape from the contingencies and enforced gregariousness of the theatre, were well served by his new media. Furthermore, many commentators have pointed out that a perfectionist is better served by recordable media than by live performance, simply because they offer the chance to preserve perfect performances for posterity, without the continued mediation of an actor. Most crucially, however, the distinctive formal issues associated with these media coincide with many of the obsessions of Beckett's writing – darkness and light, sound and silence, the nature of perception, the narration of a world into being – and generate a fruitful symbiosis between form and content.

'COMING OUT OF THE DARK': RADIO PLAYS

Beckett's plays for radio – *All That Fall* (1956); *Embers* (1958); his free adaptation of Robert Pinget's *La Manivelle* as *The Old Tune* (1960); the related subgrouping of *Words and Music* (1961), *Cascando* (1961) and *Rough for Radio I and II* (written in 1960–1, but in the case of *Rough for Radio II* not broadcast until the 1970s) – form a distinct group. Close in time and preoccupations, they mark both an end and a beginning, signalling both the end of Beckett's intensely creative 'siege in the room', and a return to English. Furthermore, they spark a major transition in his drama away from scenic location towards the non-spaces of the later drama. As *Godot* offered an escape from the suffocatingly claustrophobic and solitary world of the trilogy, the fact that the first radio play, *All That Fall*, emerged from an approach by the BBC during the final revisions to the 'difficult and elliptic' *Endgame* suggests that an escape from the stage play had become equally necessary.[2] Beckett's own account in a letter to Nancy Cunard in 1956 suggests that his interest in the idea of writing a radio play had been excited by the novelty of the medium itself. 'Never thought about a radio play technique,' he wrote, 'but in the dead of t'other night got a nicely gruesome idea full of cartwheels and dragging feet and puffing and panting which may or may not lead to something.'[3] Disembodied voices had been a feature of his fiction for years, as well as featuring in plays like *Krapp's Last Tape*, so that it seems natural he would make use of a medium in which dramas could be peopled entirely with invisible characters. In radio, Beckett continued to probe his fascination with the invisible as goad to the imagination, as well as with absence and silence counterweighting the visible and audible, as in the trademark pauses of his stage plays.

'Whenever he makes the test of a new medium, Beckett always seems to take a few steps backward,' John Spurling notes.[4] Certainly, unlike any of the later plays for radio, it would be possible, if reductive, to see *All That Fall* as a quasi-naturalistic aural drama about early twentieth-century Ireland. Indeed, various delineators of the decline of Protestants in the Irish Free State have frequently done so, without more than a nod in the direction of the play's striking strangeness, preferring instead to concentrate on its use of a genteel Hiberno-English and an investment in local colour highly uncharacteristic of Beckett.[5] The play, an atypically populous one for Beckett, is set in a recognizably Irish town named Boghill, and traces the halting progress of Maddy Rooney, a garrulous septuagenarian 'destroyed with sorrow and pining and gentility and church-going and fat and rheumatism and childlessness' (*CDW* 174), through a series of encounters with local grotesques as she goes to meet her blind husband Dan at the railway station. Clas Zilliacus has called *All That Fall* 'the passion of Maddy Rooney',[6] and certainly the play's preoccupation with faltering progress, suffering and the 'lingering dissolution' of the journey from womb to tomb suggests a kind of grotesque *via dolorosa*. Suggestions of Christ's passion are further evoked by the play's most frequent and insistent sound effect, that of *'dragging feet'*, and the characteristically Beckettian pun on station of the cross and railway station.

All That Fall, however, is a 'passion play' undermined with satire. The title derives from Psalm 145: 'The Lord upholdeth all that fall and raiseth all those that be bowed down', but, not surprisingly, the words of the psalmist are deflated throughout. The Rooneys are reduced to *'wild laughter'* at the prospect of being raised up by a divine power. Maddy is continually on the verge of stasis, of not going on, grieving specifically for her dead daughter Minnie and, more generally, as a representative of a human condition seen as irreparably fallen. All the play's characters, in fact, continually undergo misfortunes reduced to clownish pratfalls, culminating sinisterly in the reported fall of a child under the wheels of the train. The possibility of Dan Rooney's involvement in this death, given his expressed desire to 'nip some young doom in the bud' (CDW 191), sets up a muted drama of suspense in the second half of the play. However, it is one that the listener is never given enough information to resolve.

It is a characteristically Beckettian detective story, continually refusing to satisfy the desire for knowledge it generates in the auditor. We are left simply to wonder whether the ball in Dan Rooney's hand belonged to the dead child. However, plot considerations, even in this comparatively conventional play, are secondary. There are obvious parallels with *Endgame*, the play *All That Fall* most closely adjoins in time – a tyrannical blind man, with a taste for narrative and rhetoric, a doomed child, a decaying world. But where *Endgame*, despite Hamm's blindness, is a fully embodied play, here we share blindness by virtue of the medium for which *All That Fall* is written. This fact alone is more important than an implied mystery.

Beckett always refused categorically to consider *All That Fall* being presented on stage. 'Whatever quality it may have depends upon the whole thing's *coming out of the dark*,' he wrote in 1957 to his American publisher.[7] We experience the play primarily as a soundscape, a soundscape, furthermore, that does not attempt to convince the listener of its verisimilitude. Though the bulk of Maddy Rooney's 'two hundred pounds of unhealthy fat' (CDW 191) is continually insisted on throughout, and the play enjoyably elaborates upon the exertions necessary to get her into a car, we remain oddly aware that this is illusion. Maddy's grotesque body does not exist, nor the car, nor anything but the sounds of effort and exhortation. All fades into language, and that language, on Maddy's lips, has the bizarre richness of decay. Likewise, the overture of rural sounds at the beginning – '*sheep, bird, cow, cock, severally, then together*' (CDW 172) – both are flagrantly artificial radio clichés, even for 1956, and also keep reminding us of the constructed nature of what we are listening to, as the animal sounds greet Maddy's mentions of them with ludicrous promptness.

We may frequently wonder whether the entire play does not take place in Maddy's mind; the 'nightmarish quality' noted by

Martin Esslin supports his contention that the whole drama may be Maddy's bad dream.[8] The play operates along a fundamental tension, that of voices emanating from silence and returning to it, of gestures and forward movement minimally achieved over a fundamental stasis. Beckett is primarily interested in a strange condition of suspension between existence and non-existence, which makes the genteelly fading Southern Irish Protestant population an entirely apt, if uncharacteristically naturalistic, setting; radio, 'coming out of the dark', is the ideal medium in which to explore it. In radio, 'only the present speaker's presence is certain', notes Clas Zilliacus, '[and] the primary condition of existence for a radio character is that he talk'.[9] Transience, thus, is *All That Fall*'s perennial theme, appropriate in a play in which – since sound passes even as we hear it – all dwindles into silence, transient as a breath.

Beckett's next radio play, written two years after *All That Fall*, is frequently described as 'transitional'. Though still interested in the image-making capacity of the human voice, Beckett has relinquished the surface reality of *All That Fall*. It also relies more integrally on the fact that there is, in radio, nothing to see. In *Embers* (1959), the surface narrative is minimal; a bitter old solipsist talks about talking to himself, begins stories that peter out before finishing, and is haunted by voices that may be no more than the illusions of solitude. Henry's incessant gabble attempts to drown out the sound of the sea (actual or imagined, we are never sure) that operates as a tormenting amplification of his loneliness. He summons up his drowned father and estranged wife, Ada, because their 'company' is better than the self-confrontations enforced by solitude. As in *All That Fall*, Henry seems able to summon sound effects out of thin air, barking commands for hooves as though to waiting sound technicians, although his control is limited and, by the end of the play, failing. It is even more difficult than in *All That Fall* to discern what sounds or events in this aural mosaic of disembodied voices and embedded miniature narratives, flashbacks or hauntings are internal to Henry's tormented imagination.

The aural 'vacant space' of *Embers* exploits the potential for radio to play on the unverifiable, and suggests an early version

105

of the non-specific scenes of the late stage plays, with their simultaneous suggestion of interior and exterior space. Early productions of the play, for instance, gave no clue as to whether Ada and her relentlessly banal 'small chat to the babbling of Lethe' (*CDW* 265) had any existence outside Henry's head, though some later productions have decided quite clearly that Ada is a resource like Winnie's classics or handbag in *Happy Days*, to be switched on and off by Henry, rather than a physically present human being.[10] The play's effect relies on the disconcerting implications of leaking between levels, the listener's uncertainty as to where memory, haunting, fact and fiction begin and end, on the hypnotic repetition of a cluster of phrases – 'bitter cold', 'great trouble', 'white world', 'not a sound' – and the muted poignancy of the aborted story Henry tells himself, into which his stunted feelings flow. The story concerns Bolton, an 'old man in great trouble', who, awake past midnight on a 'bright winter's night, snow everywhere, bitter cold, white world' (*CDW* 254), summons his doctor, Holloway. Bolton desperately begs Holloway to perform some unspecified act, possibly euthanasia, though the nature of the agonized request is never revealed. The Bolton and Holloway story also provides the governing metaphor of the play, that of its title; the word 'embers' is repeated several times throughout the play, usually accompanied by the phrase 'not a sound'. Like the fire burnt down to embers behind Bolton, Henry's imaginative stratagems for fending off a looming nothingness, symbolized in the play by the omnipresent eerie sound of the sea, are always about to be depleted, but are never entirely exhausted.

Words and Music and *Cascando* were both written in 1961, in collaboration with Beckett's cousin, the composer John Beckett, and Marcel Mihalovici (who had previously written an opera of *Krapp's Last Tape*), respectively. Unlike *All That Fall* or *Embers*, neither play has any realistic content whatsoever. Instead, both dramas play with the self-reflexive use of recording technology. Both introduce music as a semi-autonomous character, pitting it against language in an actively adversarial relationship, as the two confront each other on the relative merits of linguistic and non-verbal modes of communication. *Words and Music* begins with Words (also known as Joe) and Music (otherwise Bob), rehearsing for a performance, and the play sees them compete with each other to satisfy their master, a crotchety impresario named Croak, by performing on the themes of 'love' and 'age'. Words firstly mouths pseudo-scholastic orotundities, but eventually evolves a muted song about a 'face in the ashes' (*CDW* 291), while Music, for its part, produces passages of music '*worthy of foregoing*' (*CDW* 288).

This points up the problem inherent in any discussion of either *Words and Music* or its sibling play *Cascando*, which sketches a similar triangular relation between Voice, Music and another impresario-figure, 'Opener'; half the 'dialogue' between words and music in both plays is missing, and without it, we cannot adjudicate between them, far less judge the truth of Beckett's reported comment to Theodor Adorno, to the effect that *Words and Music* 'ends unequivocally with the victory of the music'.[11] The play requires Music to produce melodies that should match exactly, in musical terms, Beckett's words. It is hardly surprising that none of the composers from John Beckett onward has been able to meet this impossible demand, leaving the strange competition between Words and Music rather one-sided and lacking in dramatic tension. Still, *Words and Music* and *Cascando* are interesting in that they offer most nakedly the opportunity to exploit what chiefly interested Beckett in the medium of radio. Both offer the chance to interrogate the effects achieved by alternating sound and silence, presence and absence, the peopling and dispeopling of the listener's sound-space, between 'going on' and lapsing into dead air.

FILM

Beckett's one foray into film resulted, like his first radio drama, from a commission. In 1963, Beckett's American publisher, Barney Rosset, decided to expand into film production and invited Beckett, along with Harold Pinter and Eugène Ionesco, to write something for the medium. Again, as with radio, Beckett's alacrity in composing a screenplay demonstrated his fascination with, and knowledge of, film. (As a young man he had asked the Russian director Sergei Eisenstein to take him on as an assistant.[12]) *Film*, produced by Evergreen Theatre in

107

1964 and starring Buster Keaton in his last film role, was shot in 35mm black and white under the direction of Alan Schneider. It is a strikingly strange artefact, with a twenty-two-minute running time like the experimental shorts of the dada and surrealist film-makers. It stars an actor Beckett admired for his 1920s comedy, is silent apart from a single 'sssh!' (by which Beckett humorously conveys that *Film* is silent by choice, or for reasons of silent-screen *hommage*, not for want of technical resources), and combines elements of broad slapstick with Berkeleyan philosophy.

Film is, as Linda Ben-Zvi writes, 'a film about film'.[13] Like *Play*, its generic title indicates that, rather than using the medium as an inconspicuous or transparent mode of telling a story about something else, the work will be in some sense a meditation on the fundamental traits of its medium. The screenplay, with its detailed notes – itself a curious text, combining potted philosophy, copious diagramming and passages of some of the most uninflected narrative encountered anywhere in Beckett – admits more than once to an ignorance of technical issues. *Film*, however, is also an extremely knowing piece of work. Jonathan Kalb points out its debt to the French New Wave of the early 1960s, with which it shares many formal concerns, including a self-reflexive concern with the camera-as-eye, the use or invocation of a Hollywood icon, and a general display of knowledge of the history of film, among others.[14] The close-ups of Keaton's blinking reptilian eye, for instance, are among a network of references to Luis Bunuel's *Un chien andalou*, first shown in Paris in 1928, and whose script appeared in the same 1932 issue of the special surrealist issues of the journal *This Quarter* as Beckett's translations of Crevel, Eluard and Breton.[15]

The action of *Film* seems simple to the point of banality. One critic describes it as a 'Keystone Cops'-style chase in what Beckett specified should be a *'comic and unreal'* ambiance.[16] This chase, however, takes place between O (Object) and E (Eye), which are eventually revealed as *'sundered'* elements of the single protagonist, a dark-coated, wall-hugging paranoiac, with an eye-patch like a pirate's, played by Keaton. Throughout most of the film, E is the camera, O the human object on-screen, frantically fleeing, in *'comic foundered precipitancy'*

108

(*CDW* 324) from the gaze that exposes him to the ultimate horror, the *'anguish of perceivedness'* (*CDW* 323). O tries to remove all perception – cloaking himself in the characteristic Beckett garb of hat and overcoat, hugging a wall on the street, escaping into an illusory sanctuary – an attempt that ultimately fails, because he cannot, in the end, escape self-perception.

Over its three parts, *Film* moves from the public arena ('the street', with surreal-looking couples in summer clothes encountering the great-coated Keaton *'hastening blindly'* by a wall) to the private ('*the room'*), via *'the stairs'*. '*The room'* focuses on O after he attempts to relax into a false sanctuary, where he is able, in an extended comic sequence, to cover or eject anything capable of seeing. (This includes window, mirror, cat, dog, parrot, goldfish, a print of 'God the Father', even an envelope whose round fasteners resemble eyes.) He also examines and destroys in chronological order a set of photographs of himself at seven stages of his life, from infancy to dour middle age. Having apparently made the room safe, O falls asleep, only for E to manœuvre into a position to be able to stare him nakedly in the face, and reveal the full-face view we have been denied till now. Finally, O awakes and comes literally face to face with the agonizing realization that the *'pursuing perceiver is not extraneous, but self'* (*CDW* 323).

The original title was 'The Eye' and the epigraph tells us that the work, with its fascination with the technology of the camera lens, is based on the philosopher George Berkeley's dictum that *esse est percipi,* to be is to be perceived. The world, for Berkeley (1685–1753), has no existence outside the perceiving mind, which exists in its turn only because perceived by an all-seeing God. In his notes to the screenplay, however, Beckett undercuts the statement as soon as he makes it by noting that 'no truth value attaches to above, regarded as of merely structural and dramatic convenience' (*CDW* 323). As with Beckett's dismissal of overtly Christian interpretations of *Waiting for Godot, Film* dismisses the Christian notion of God as a comforting guarantee of perception. Instead, it mounts an exploration of the horrors of self-scrutiny, although it has generated some commentary suggesting that E becomes a kind of God surrogate 'in a world in which God no longer perceives'.[17] Other readings have highlighted the imperfect

109

perceptions of both O and E, and suggested that Beckett's project is to emphasize the fallen nature of non-divine perception. It has generated criticism reading it as a parable about lack of unity in the self, and the impossibility of perfect self-identity or self-knowledge, the problem of clearly seeing an 'I', the validity of subject/object distinctions, a meditation on scopophilia, or the invasiveness of technologies of seeing. Dispensing with the verbal, and substituting, as Hugh Kenner points out, for the 'ineluctable voice' of *Embers* the 'ineluctable eye' that would also feature in *Eh Joe*,[18] *Film* is about the process of watching and looking, an elaboration on the eye/I pun he would also explore in *Not I*.

'FAMILIAR CHAMBERS': TELEVISION PLAYS

By the time he began to write for television, Beckett had already established a reputation for consistently frustrating the expectations of genre. Television is enormously powerful, and Beckett used it to continue his probing of powerlessness, ignorance and impotence. As a writer for television, Beckett explores its shadowy potential to disrupt. His methods develop from his disquieting transposition of some of the preoccupations of *Embers* to the small screen in *Eh Joe* (1965) and *Ghost Trio* (1976), to the brevity and wordlessness of the dramas of the early 1980s, with their clear affinities with both the *Words and Music* cycle of radio plays, and ritualistic late stage dramas such as *Footfalls* and *Rockaby*. While cinema isolates and enlarges – we watch oversized images in the dark, in a place removed from everyday concerns – television brings its images into the living room, shortening the distance between the audience and the object under scrutiny. With their frequent self-conscious theatricality – the sidestepped melodrama of *Eh Joe*, the deliberate use of studio sound effects in *Ghost Trio* – these plays were written to stage a disturbing revision of television cliché in a medium typically watched by passively expectant viewers isolated, like the protagonists, in their own intimate spaces.

Written in 1965 for the actor Jack McGowran, *Eh Joe* is the earliest of Beckett's plays for television by a decade. It presents what Rosette Lamont calls a 'small-screen haiku on the subject

110

of love's death-dealing failure'.[19] The protagonist Joe is a grey-haired, dressing-gowned figure seen sitting alone on his bed. Another avatar of *Embers'* Henry, he fears and craves the sound of a tormenting woman's 'flint glass' voice, which harangues him for past failure. Voice accuses Joe of womanizing, infidelity and cruelty, and, in particular, indicts his callous treatment of a girl who committed suicide after he had left her. *Eh Joe* clarifies and renders explicit some elements of *Embers* by letting one voice – low and remote, a version of Ada – aggressively haunt a solitary protagonist in a less enigmatic, more remorseless work, which imprisons Joe's unspeaking head on screen for an eternity during which voice and camera assault him in concert. We hear what Joe hears; the *'low, distinct, remote'* voice, apparently that of a former lover, with its insinuating, hypnotic refrain of 'Eh Joe?' However, what we see, after Joe makes his brief survey of the room, as though to ensure he is alone, is a precise choreography of nine camera movements in increasing close-up on Joe's face, *'say four inches each time'* (CDW 361). The camera records his impassive face, still *'except insofar as it reflects mounting tension of listening'* (CDW 362), one of the primary dramatic situations Beckett would work with throughout the rest of his career as a dramatist in all media.

Eh Joe is a transitional work, in which Beckett is still using the camera as a hostile hounding device, as in *Film*, but the setting has moved entirely to one of the many individual chambers that will feature in the later television plays. Also, after the silence of *Film*, language has returned, malicious and accusatory, in the shape of Voice's twenty-minute invective from 'behind the eyes' (CDW 363), apparently the final vengeful remnant of what was once a chorus of haunting voices. The frenetic movement of *Film* has gone, not to return in the television plays, and is replaced by the juxtaposition of a spoken text with a relatively static visual image, goading the viewer to ask questions about their ambiguous interrelation. If Voice's story of sex, suicide and remorse is, as some critics have found it, crude and melodramatic, *Eh Joe's* originality rests in its use of a new medium to metaphorize, via a banal tale of love and betrayal, its protagonist's descent into a kind of *crise de conscience*.

111

Beckett's work had taken enormous strides by the time he wrote his next television play, *Ghost Trio*, a decade later in 1975. It was broadcast along with . . . *but the clouds* . . . in April 1977 as a three-part programme collectively called *Shades*, along with the TV adaptation of the stage play *Not I*. He had written *Not I*, *That Time* and *Footfalls* of his late stage plays, all of which were composed in a relationship of complex mutual influence with the television plays from *Ghost Trio* onward. The influence of the stage plays on the television plays and vice versa can be seen most obviously in their abandonment of the relative naturalism still governing *Eh Joe*. Instead, all take an interest in presenting mysterious tableaux in ambiguous relationships to spoken monologues, and in an increasing presentation of figures who are not only ephemeral, but possibly dead, or existing in some kind of purgatorial afterlife (the urn-bound heads in *Play*, May in *Footfalls*, who is 'not quite there').

Ghost Trio, while set again in what it calls 'the familiar chamber' known to the viewer from *Eh Joe*, is more involved with the evocative nature of its musical structure than with communicating any residual trace of dramatic plot. Mysterious and unearthly, the play is set to excerpts from Beethoven's Fifth Piano Trio, op. 70, known as *The Ghost*, composed for an opera based on *Macbeth*. The music, particular passages of which are specified in the screenplay, becomes as much a protagonist in the unfolding drama of the angular room in 'shades of grey' (*CDW* 408) as the waiting of the male figure F, the quiet, sometimes sardonic commands of the female V and the camera that obeys her. The minimal action depicts F apparently thwarted in his expectation of a visit, possibly from the woman whose faint and unimpassioned voice directs camera and viewer to 'look again'. An earlier title for the play was *Tryst*, but, as in *Waiting for Godot*, this tryst will not occur, and, as in *Godot*, the viewer asks questions about the identity of V – is she the expected visitor, a reluctant muse, F's anima or, as James Knowlson suggests, a female Death who will not release F from his death-in-life?[20] What we finally see through the door, in the third part of the play, after V has fallen silent, but in which F continues his soundless activities, is a boy – both the self-referential ghost of *Godot*'s Boy and a tissue of

112

other theatre ghosts like Hamlet's father and *Macbeth*'s Banquo. The Boy simply *'shakes head faintly'* and departs, leaving F to the titular 'ghost trio', the haunting combination of music, voice and camera, directing and animating the movements of an actor reduced, for the most part, to a stage prop. From *Ghost Trio* onward, Beckett's television plays move towards abstraction. They rely increasingly on voices that have moved out of characters' heads and become impersonal masters of ceremonies, and on musical, mathematical and poetic motifs repeated in muted 'shades of grey' (*CDW* 408).

Beckett's poetics of television technology can be seen in . . . *but the clouds* . . . in even sharper relief. The play, written in 1976 and broadcast along with *Ghost Trio* by the BBC in 1977, uses some of the same technical devices as the earlier play, with Yeats's poem replacing Beethoven's music. . . . *but the clouds* . . . takes its title and the theme on which it works a variation from the sonorous final stanza of 'The Tower', which Beckett could recite from memory:

> Now shall I make my soul,
> Compelling it to study
> In a learned school
> Till the wreck of body,
> Slow decay of blood,
> Testy delirium
> Or dull decrepitude
> Or what worse evil come –
> The death of friends, or death
> Of every brilliant eye
> That made a catch in the breath –
> Seem but the clouds of the sky
> When the horizon fades,
> Or a bird's sleepy cry
> Among the deepening shades.[21]

As Martin Esslin has suggested, the play draws much of its muted vitality from Paul Valéry's concept of the *ligne donnée*, the given line on which another imagination imposes its will.[22] Here Beckett takes on a poem that deals dauntlessly with 'soul making', the ageing speaker's truce with the prospect and actuality of old age and death, and the rapture of a final frenzy of writing in the very teeth of death. Yeats, by the sheer force

113

of his rhetoric, is almost successful in convincing the reader that the final transport of soul making makes the death of loved ones seem an ephemeral loss. Beckett, as one would expect of the author of *Krapp's Last Tape*, cannot accept this major chord, and leans his own television play antagonistically against Yeats's lines.

... but the clouds ... shows us a man bent over a table, and moving in and out of a lighted circle surrounded by darkness, putting on his nightclothes, then crouching in order to 'beg, of her, to appear', these activities narrated by his recorded voice (V). A woman's face (W), presumably a lost loved one, appears briefly on the screen whenever V speaks of summoning her, reciting the closing lines of the Yeats poem inaudibly along with V (*CDW* 409). Among other things, W is presumably a version of the archetypal 'woman lost' on which the speaker of 'The Tower' claims the imagination 'dwell[s] the most'; Yeats's speaker turned aside from pursuing her through 'pride | Cowardice, some silly, over-subtle thought', and her recurring memory is dreadful because so poignant. In *... but the clouds ...* , however, whereas Yeats's speaker rises to the compensatory creation of 'Translunar Paradise' in his art, Beckett's character departs as he arrives, with no revelation. For Beckett's M, there is no tower and no Byzantium, only a fading horizon of memory and some few embers in the 'deepening shades'.

Beckett's two final television plays, *Nacht und Träume* and *Quad*, mark a complete break with words. *Nacht und Träume* contains only a seven-bar sung fragment of one of Schubert's *lieder*, and *Quad* consists entirely of wordless action. Both offer instances of him working in ways that more closely resemble painting or choreography than play-writing. *Nacht und Träume* resembles *... but the clouds ...* in its evocation of a nighttime vision visiting a solitary protagonist. This time, though, there is not even a minimal narrative voiceover, simply a series of tableaux, accompanied by a male voice lulling the protagonist to sleep with 'Hölde Träume, kehret wieder' ('Lovely dreams, come again') from Schubert's *Nacht und Träume* ('Night and Dreams'). We then see Dreamer's dream self being visited by disembodied hands, which offer him a chalice, wipe his brow and cushion his head, a sequence of movements then repeated

114

in extreme close-up, like a set of Old Masters animated eerily for television (*CDW* 465). *Quad*, relinquishing even this residual use of words in favour of movement, light and percussion, is nonetheless a powerful culmination of Beckett's work for television. Four players in long gowns and cowls ritually pace a square lighted area in rhythmic movement, swerving away from the centre, which is termed a *'danger zone'* by the script (*CDW* 453). The effect is, as S. E. Gontarski dubs it, one of 'prescribed, determined, enforced motion',[23] suggesting both Newton's laws of motion and the Cartesian ideal of the self-regulating machine. The pacing figures, each accompanied by a different form of percussion, seem to be cogs in an impersonal mechanism, while their ritual movement in monk-like robes, inscribing patterns around an unknown centre, suggests attempts to control fear, a dance or wordless prayer to appease the gods.

Quad, in its brevity and wordlessness, nevertheless suggests a culmination or concretization of themes from a wide range of previous Beckett works. The emergence of the players out of darkness and their return to it suggest the impersonal procession from birth to death, womb to tomb, which is a perennial Beckett theme, while the feverish monotony of their ritual is reminiscent of various Dantean overtones from a multitude of other Beckett dramas, as well as the ritual rocking and walking of *Footfalls* and *Rockaby*. Suggesting, as Phyllis Carey argues, a deliberate attempt at 'enframing the invisible', *Quad* sees Beckett abandoning his long struggle with a recalcitrant language for a silent contemplation of being.[24]

Notes

PROLOGUE

1. 'Samuel Beckett: Moody Man of Letters', interview with Israel Shenker, *New York Times*, 6 May 1956, Sect. 2, 3.
2. Tom Driver, 'Beckett by the Madeleine', *Columbia University Forum*, 4 (Summer 1961), 21–5, 23.

CHAPTER 1. 'DIFFICULT MUSIC': THE EARLY FICTION

1. Charles Juliet, 'Meeting Beckett', trans. Suzanne Chamier, *Tri-Quarterly*, 77 (1989–90), 22.
2. Letter to Eoin O'Brien, quoted in 'Introduction', *Dream of Fair to Middling Women*, ed. Eoin O'Brien and Edith Fournier (Dublin: Black Cat Press, 1992), x.
3. John Pilling, 'Beckett's English Fiction', in *The Cambridge Companion to Samuel Beckett* (Cambridge: Cambridge University Press, 1994), 20.
4. 'Saul, Saul, why persecutest thou me? ... I am Jesus whom thou persecutest: It is hard for thee to kick against the pricks' (Acts 9: 4–5).
5. *The Spectator*, 25 March 1938, 546.
6. Hugh Kenner, *A Reader's Guide to Samuel Beckett* (London: Thames & Hudson, 1973), 57.
7. Quoted in John Fletcher, *The Novels of Samuel Beckett* (London: Chatto & Windus, 1964), 59.
8. For more on bilingual pressures in *Watt*, see Ann Beer, 'Beckett's Bilingualism', in *Cambridge Companion to Beckett*, 209–21.
9. Leslie Hill, *Beckett's Fiction: In Different Words* (Cambridge: Cambridge University Press, 1990), 23.
10. Kenner, *A Reader's Guide*, 57.
11. A. Alvarez, *Beckett* (London: Fontana, 1973), 43.

116

12. 'Tailpiece', in *Collected Poems 1930–1978* (London: John Calder, 1984), 170.
13. Steven Connor, *Samuel Beckett: Repetition, Theory and Text* (Oxford: Basil Blackwell, 1988), 158 ff.

CHAPTER 2. BOTCHED AUTOBIOGRAPHIES: THE TRILOGY

1. Hugh Kenner formulated this phrase in his *Samuel Beckett* (New York: Grove Press, 1961), 21.
2. Beckett's 1957 comment that 'there is something in English writing that infuriates me and I can't get rid of it. A kind of lack of brakes' is quoted in Clas Zilliacus, *Beckett and Broadcasting: A Study of the Works of Samuel Beckett for and in Radio and Television* (Abo: Abo Akademi, 1976), 149. His 1962 comment to Israel Shenker about writing in French being 'more exciting' is in an interview entitled 'Moody Man of Letters', *New York Times*, 6 May 1962, Sect. 2, 3. His statement to Richard Coe that he was afraid of English 'because you couldn't help writing poetry in it' and to Niklaus Gessner about the possibility of writing 'sans style' (without style) in French are quoted in Richard Coe, *Beckett* (rev. edn., New York: Grove Press, 1968), 14.
3. See e.g. Marjorie Perloff, ' "Une voix pas la mienne": French/English Beckett and the French/English Reader', in her *Poetic Licence: Essays on Modernist and Postmodernist Lyric* (Evanston, Ill.: Northwestern University Press, 1990), 161–73. Perloff reads Beckett's desire to write 'without style' in his adopted language as a wish to get beyond the influence of Joycean style in particular, and also, more generally, the legacy of Shakespeare, Milton and the Romantic and Victorian poets.
4. Eric P. Levy, *Beckett and the Voice of Species* (Dublin: Gill and Macmillan; Totowa, NJ: Barnes and Noble, 1980), 54.
5. Hugh Kenner, *A Reader's Guide to Samuel Beckett* (London: Thames & Hudson, 1973), 97.
6. Andrew Kennedy, *Samuel Beckett* (Cambridge: Cambridge University Press, 1989), 114.
7. Daniel Albright, *Representation and Imagination: Beckett, Kafka, Nobokov and Schoenberg* (Chicago: University of Chicago Press, 1981), 186.
8. See Edouard Morot-Sir, 'Grammatical Insincerity in *The Unnamable*', in Harold Bloom (ed.), *Samuel Beckett's* Molloy, Malone Dies, The Unnamable (New York: Chelsea House Publishers, 1988), 131–44, for an illuminating discussion of this notion.

CHAPTER 3. FEARFUL SYMMETRIES *WAITING FOR GODOT* TO *PLAY*

1. Jacques Lemarchand, review of *Waiting for Godot*, repr. in Peter Boxall (ed.), *Samuel Beckett: Waiting for Godot, Endgame* (Duxford: Icon, 2000), 10.
2. Kenneth Tynan, review of *Waiting for Godot*, repr. in ibid., 11.
3. Eric Bentley, 'An Anti-Play', in Ruby Cohn (ed.), *Samuel Beckett: Waiting for Godot: A Casebook* (Basingstoke: Macmillan Education, 1987), 23 ff.
4. Vivian Mercier, 'The Mathematical Limit', *The Nation* (14 Feb. 1959), 144–5.
5. Repr. in Cohn, *Samuel Beckett: Waiting for Godot: A Casebook*, 173.
6. Geneviève Serreau, *Histoire du 'nouveau théâtre'* (Paris: Gallimard, 1966), 90.
7. Lawrence Graver, *Beckett: Waiting for Godot* (Cambridge and New York: Cambridge University Press, 1989).
8. Quoted in Raymond Federman and John Fletcher, *Samuel Beckett: The Critical Heritage* (London: Routledge & Kegan Paul, 1979), 10.
9. Alan Schneider, 'Waiting for Beckett', in John Calder (ed.), *Beckett at Sixty: A Festschrift* (London: Calder & Boyars, 1967), 38.
10. A. Alvarez, *Beckett* (London: Fontana, 1973), 94–5.
11. Michael Worton, '*Waiting for Godot* and *Endgame*: Theatre as Text', in *The Cambridge Companion to Beckett* (Cambridge: Cambridge University Press, 1994), 71.
12. 'The key word in my plays is perhaps', in Tom Driver, 'Beckett by the Madeleine', *Columbia University Forum*, 4 (Summer 1961), 21–5, 23.
13. Israel Shenker, 'Samuel Beckett: Moody Man of Letters', interview, *New York Times*, 6 May 1956, Sect. 2, 3.
14. Vivian Mercier, 'How to read *Endgame*', in Cathleen Culotta Andonian (ed.), *The Critical Response to Samuel Beckett* (Westport, Conn., and London: Greenwood Press, 1998), 114–17.
15. Harold Clurman, review of *Endgame*, repr. in ibid., 118–20, 118.
16. Per Nykrog, 'In the Ruins of the Past: Reading Beckett Intertextually', in ibid., 120–41, 135.
17. Hugh Kenner, *A Reader's Guide to Samuel Beckett* (London: Thames & Hudson, 1973), 122.
18. Quoted in Ruby Cohn, *Back to Beckett* (Princeton: Princeton University Press, 1973), 152.
19. Andrew Kennedy, *Samuel Beckett* (Cambridge: Cambridge University Press, 1989), 69.
20. Alvarez, *Beckett*, 115.
21. Paul Lawley, 'Stages of Identity: from *Krapp's Last Tape* to *Play*', in *The Cambridge Companion to Beckett*, 95.

22. Terry Eagleton, 'Beckett's Paradoxes', in *Crazy John and the Bishop* (Cork: Cork University Press in association with Field Day, 1998), 302.
23. Tom Driver, 'Beckett by the Madeleine', Columbia University Forum, 4 (Summer 1961), 21–5, 23.

CHAPTER 4. 'GHOST ROOMS': THE LATE THEATRE

1. Deirdre Bair, *Samuel Beckett* (London: Jonathan Cape, 1978), 544.
2. In fact, despite Beckett's sense of gratitude to Tynan, who had been one of the first champions of the London *Godot*, the affair ended badly, after 'naked bodies' had been added to the 'miscellaneous rubbish', and Beckett's anonymity was violated in an illustrated book accompanying the production. See James Knowlson, *Damned to Fame: A Life of Samuel Beckett* (London: Bloomsbury, 1996), 565–6.
3. A. Alvarez, *Beckett* (London: Fontana, 1973), 141.
4. Enoch Brater, *Beyond Minimalism: Beckett's Late Style in the Theatre* (New York and Oxford: Oxford University Press, 1987), 37.
5. See e.g. Mary Bryden, *Women in Samuel Beckett's Prose and Drama* (Houndmills: Macmillan, 1993) and Linda Ben-Zvi (ed.), *Women in Beckett: Performance and Critical Perspectives* (Urbana, Ill.: University of Illinois Press, 1992).
6. Bryden, *Women in Samuel Beckett's Prose and Drama*, 114.
7. Andrew Kennedy, 'Mutations of the Soliloquy – *Not I* to *Rockaby*', in Robin J. Davis and Lance St J. Butler (eds.), *Make Sense Who May: Essays on Samuel Beckett's Later Works* (Gerrards Cross: Colin Smythe, 1988), 30–5, 30.
8. Ibid.
9. Brater, *Beyond Minimalism*, 18.
10. Interview with Jessica Tandy, quoted in ibid., 23.
11. BBC filmed *Not I* in 1976. For technical reasons, it was impossible to replicate the effects of the Auditor and Mouth, so the BBC received Beckett's permission to focus in a single long close-up on Mouth alone, rendering the swooping distant butterfly of the stage version to a unambiguously vaginal image.
12. Keir Elam, 'Dead Heads: Damnation-Narration in the "Dramaticules"', in *The Cambridge Companion to Beckett* (Cambridge: Cambridge University Press, 1994), 145–66, 153.
13. Hélène L. Baldwin, *Samuel Beckett's Real Silence* (University Park, Pa., and London: Pennsylvania State University Press, 1981), 136–42.
14. Mary A. Doll, 'Walking and Rocking: Ritual Acts in *Footfalls* and *Rockaby*', in Davis and Butler (eds.), *Make Sense Who May*, 46–55.
15. Bryden, *Women in Samuel Beckett's Prose and Drama*, 115.

16. *Footfalls* is generally thought to have its root in the lecture by Jung at London's Tavistock Clinic, which Beckett attended with his analyst Wilfred Bion in September 1935. An anecdote told by Jung about a young female patient who 'had never been born entirely' seems to have caught Beckett's imagination, since it also features more explicitly in the 1956 radio play *All That Fall*, and appears to have been the crystallization of the deep-seated womb fixation that features so frequently in his work. See Knowlson, *Damned to Fame*, 175 ff.

17. Anna McMullan, *Theatre on Trial: Samuel Beckett's Later Drama* (London: Routledge, 1993), 96.

18. Charles R. Lyons, 'Perceiving *Rockaby* as a Text, as a Text by Samuel Beckett, as a Text for Performance', *Comparative Drama*, 16/4 (1982), 305–15, 307.

19. Bryden, *Women in Beckett's Prose and Drama*, 120–1.

20. Brater, *Beyond Minimalism*, 172.

21. Quoted in ibid., 173.

22. Ibid., 113.

23. Ibid., 116.

24. Pierre Astier, 'Beckett's *Ohio Impromptu*: A View from the Isle of Swans', *Modern Drama*, 25/3 (1982), 332.

25. McMullan, *Theatre on Trial*, 119.

26. Havel's subversive activities included his membership of the Committee for the Defence of the Unjustly Persecuted (VONS) and his signing of the Charter 77 manifesto. He would read the plays only after he had left prison; he wrote a response to *Catastrophe* called *Mistake*, and English translations of both were printed together in the *Index on Censorship* for February 1984, and appeared as a double bill in the Stockholm Stadstheater in 1983. Beckett's English *Catastrophe* had already appeared in the *New Yorker* in early 1983. See Knowlson, *Damned to Fame*, 677 ff.

27. Martin Esslin, 'Visions of Absence: Beckett's *Footfalls*, *Ghost Trio* and . . . *but the clouds* . . .', in Ian Donaldson (ed.), *Transformations in Modern European Drama* (Atlantic Highlands, NJ: Humanities Press, 1983), 112–22.

CHAPTER 5. 'FANCY DEAD': THE POST-TRILOGY PROSE

1. Samuel Beckett, letter to his American publisher Barney Rosset, dated 11 January 1954, quoted in S. E. Gontarski, 'Introduction', *Samuel Beckett: The Complete Short Prose 1929–1989*, ed. S. E. Gontarski (New York: Grove Press, 1995), p. xiv.

2. H. Porter Abbott, 'Beginning Again: The Post-Narrative Art of *Texts for Nothing* and *How It Is*', in *The Cambridge Companion to Beckett* (Cambridge: Cambridge University Press, 1994), 107–8.

3. Robert Cochran, *Samuel Beckett: A Study of the Short Fiction* (New York: Twayne, 1991), 35.
4. Hugh Kenner, *A Reader's Guide to Samuel Beckett* (London: Thames & Hudson, 1973), 136–46.
5. The dimensions of the cylinder of *The Lost Ones* have altered from edition to edition. See S. E. Gontarski, 'Note on the Texts', in *Complete Short Prose*, 282–3, for an overview.
6. A. Alvarez, *Beckett* (London: Fontana, 1973), 136.
7. Cochran, *A Study of the Short Fiction*, 55–6.
8. *Six Residua* (London: John Calder, 1978) includes *From and Abandoned Work*, *Enough*, *Imagination Dead Imagine*, *Ping*, *Lessness* and *The Lost Ones*.
9. See Gontarski, 'Introduction', p. xii; see also his 'Note on the Texts', 279–86, for a comprehensive account of the evolution and publication history of the late prose.
10. Quoted in Gontarski, 'Introduction', p. xv.
11. Brian Wicker, 'Samuel Beckett and the Death of the God-Narrator', *Journal of Narrative Technique*, 4/1 (Jan. 1974), 62–74, 71.
12. Andrew Renton, 'Disabled Figures: From the *Residua* to *Stirrings Still*', *The Cambridge Companion to Beckett*, 170.
13. Gontarski, 'Introduction', p. xv.
14. Kenner, *A Reader's Guide*, 179.
15. Alvarez, *Beckett*, 133.
16. John Pilling, ' "Company" by Samuel Beckett', *Journal of Beckett Studies*, 7 (Spring 1982), 127.
17. Cochran, *A Study of the Short Fiction*, 70.
18. H. Porter Abbott, *Beckett Writing Beckett: the Author in the Autograph* (Ithaca, NY, and London: Cornell University Press, 1996), 18–19.
19. Leo Bersani and Ulysse Dutoit, 'Beckett's Sociability', in Cathleen Culotta Andonian (ed.), *Critical Response to Samuel Beckett*, 176–83, 183.
20. The account of Beckett's relationship with his mother is at its most baroque in Bair, but is documented with sympathy in Anthony Cronin, *Samuel Beckett: The Last Modernist* (London: Harper Collins, 1996), especially 17 ff.
21. Alvarez, *Beckett*, 82.

CHAPTER 6. SCREENS AND SOUNDS: RADIO, FILM AND TELEVISION DRAMA

1. See Jonathan Kalb, 'The Mediated Quixote: The Radio and Television Plays, and *Film*', in *Cambridge Companion to Beckett* (Cambridge: Cambridge University Press, 1994), 124–5.

2. Letter from Samuel Beckett to Alan Schneider, quoted in Deirdre Bair, *Samuel Beckett* (London: Jonathan Cape, 1978), 464.
3. Quoted in Katherine Worth, 'Beckett and the Radio Medium', in John Drakakis (ed.), *British Radio Drama* (Cambridge: Cambridge University Press, 1981), 197.
4. John Fletcher and John Spurling, *Beckett the Playwright* (London: Methuen, 1985), 44.
5. Kalb, 'The Mediated Quixote', 126.
6. Clas Zilliacus, *Beckett and Broadcasting: A Study of the Works of Samuel Beckett for and in Radio and Television* (Abo: Abo Akademi, 1976), 137.
7. Quoted in ibid., 3.
8. Martin Esslin, *Mediations: Essays on Brecht, Beckett and the Media* (New York: Grove Press, 1982), 131.
9. Zilliacus, *Beckett and Broadcasting*, 56.
10. See Kalb, 'The Mediated Quixote', 130.
11. Quoted in Zilliacus, *Beckett and Broadcasting*, 114.
12. See James Knowlson, *Damned to Fame: A Life of Samuel Beckett* (London: Bloomsbury, 1996), 226.
13. Linda Ben-Zvi, 'Samuel Beckett's Media Plays', *Modern Drama*, 28/1 (Mar. 1985), 22–37.
14. Kalb, 'The Mediated Quixote', 134.
15. *This Quarter*, 5 (1932).
16. Ben-Zvi, 'Samuel Beckett's Media Plays', 30.
17. Vincent Murphy, 'Being and Perception: Beckett's *Film*', *Modern Drama*, 18/1 (Mar. 975), 43–8.
18. Hugh Kenner, *A Reader's Guide to Samuel Beckett* (London: Thames & Hudson, 1973), 167.
19. Rosette Lamont, 'Beckett's *Eh Joe*: Lending an Ear to the Anima', in Linda Ben-Zvi (ed.), *Women in Beckett: Performance and Critical Perspectives* (Urbana, Ill.: University of Illinois Press, 1992), 228–35, 228.
20. James Knowlson, '*Ghost Trio/Geister Trio*', in Enoch Brater (ed.), *Beckett at 80/Beckett in Context* (New York and Oxford: Oxford University Press, 1986), 193–207.
21. *The Collected Poems of W. B. Yeats* (New York: Macmillan, 1959), 197.
22. Esslin, *Mediations: Essays on Brecht, Beckett and the Media*, 132.
23. S. E. Gontarski, 'Review: *Quad* I and II, Beckett's sinister mimes', *Journal of Beckett Studies* 9 (1984), 137.
24. Phyllis Carey, 'The *Quad* Pieces: A Screen for the Unseeable', in R. J. Davis and L. St J. Butler (eds.), *Make Sense Who May*, 145–9, 148.

Select Bibliography

PRIMARY WORKS BY SAMUEL BECKETT

Details of the first editions in English of Beckett's work are given below. When the first edition is in French, it is followed by details of the first English edition.

Collected Poems 1930–1978 (London: John Calder, 1984).

The Complete Dramatic Works (London and Boston: Faber & Faber, 1986).

The Complete Short Prose 1929–1989, ed. S. E. Gontarski (New York: Grove Press, 1995).

Our Exagmination Round his Factification for Incamination of Work in Progress, by Samuel Beckett and others (Paris: Shakespeare and Co., 1929).

Whoroscope (Paris: The Hours Press, 1930).

Proust (London: Chatto & Windus, 1931).

More Pricks Than Kicks (London: Chatto & Windus, 1934).

Echo's Bones and Other Precipitates (Paris: Europa Press, 1935).

Murphy (London: G. Routledge, 1938).

Molloy (Paris: Éditions de Minuit, 1951). *Molloy*, trans. Samuel Beckett and Patrick Bowles (Paris: Olympia Press, 1955).

Malone meurt (Paris: Éditions de Minuit, 1951). *Malone Dies* (London: John Calder, 1958).

En attendant Godot (Paris: Éditions de Minuit, 1952). *Waiting for Godot* (London: Faber & Faber, 1956).

L'Innommable (Paris: Éditions de Minuit, 1953). *The Unnamable* (London: John Calder, 1959).

Watt (Paris: Olympia Press, 1953).

Nouvelles et textes pour rien (Paris: Éditions de Minuit, 1955). Translations in *No's Knife* (London: Calder & Boyars, 1967).

All That Fall (London: Faber & Faber, 1957).

Fin de partie suivie de Acte sans paroles (Paris: Éditions de Minuit, 1957). *Endgame. Followed by Act Without Words* (London: Faber & Faber, 1958).

Krapp's Last Tape and Embers (London: Faber & Faber, 1959).
Comment c'est (Paris: Éditions de Minuit, 1961). *How It Is* (London: John Calder, 1964).
Poems in English (London: John Calder, 1961).
Happy Days (London: Faber & Faber, 1962).
Play and Two Short Pieces for Radio (London: Faber & Faber, 1964).
Imagination morte imaginez (Paris: Éditions de Minuit, 1965). *Imagination Dead Imagine* (London: Calder & Boyars, 1965).
Assez (Paris: Éditions de Minuit, 1966). *Enough* in *No's Knife*.
Bing (Paris: Éditions de Minuit, 1966). *Ping* in *No's Knife*.
Come and Go (London: Calder & Boyars, 1967).
Eh Joe and Other Writings (London: Faber & Faber, 1967).
No's Knife: Collected Shorter Prose 1945–1966 (London: Calder & Boyars, 1967).
From an Abandoned Work. In *No's Knife*.
Sans (Paris: Éditions de Minuit, 1969). *Lessness* (London: Calder & Boyars, 1970).
Mercier et Camier (Paris: Éditions de Minuit, 1970). *Mercier and Camier* (London: Calder & Boyars, 1974).
Premier amour (Paris: Éditions de Minuit, 1970). *First Love* (London: Calder & Boyars, 1973).
Le Dépeupleur (Paris: Éditions de Minuit, 1970). *The Lost Ones* (London: Calder & Boyars, 1972).
Not I (London: Faber & Faber, 1973).
Still (London: Calder & Boyars, 1975).
All Strange Away (New York: Gotham Book Mart, 1976).
Pour finir encore et autres foirades (Paris: Éditions de Minuit, 1976). *For To End Yet Again and Other Fizzles* (London: John Calder, 1976).
That Time (London: Faber & Faber, 1976).
Footfalls (London: Faber & Faber, 1976).
Ends and Odds (London: Faber & Faber, 1977).
Collected Poems in English and French (London: John Calder, 1977).
Company (London: John Calder, 1979).
Mal vu mal dit (Paris: Éditions de Minuit, 1981). *Ill Seen Ill Said* (London: John Calder, 1982).
Rockaby and Other Short Pieces (London: Faber & Faber, 1982).
Catastrophe et autres dramaticules (Paris: Éditions de Minuit, 1982). *Catastrophe* (London: Faber & Faber, 1984).
Worstward Ho (London: John Calder, 1983).
Disjecta. Miscellaneous Writings and a Dramatic Fragment, ed. Ruby Cohn (London: John Calder, 1983).
Collected Shorter Plays (London: Faber & Faber, 1984).
Stirrings Still, illustrated by Louis le Broquy (New York: Blue Moon Books; London: John Calder, 1988).
Collected Shorter Prose 1945–80 (London: John Calder, 1988).

Nohow On (London: John Calder, 1989).
As the Story Was Told: Uncollected and Late Prose (London: John Calder, 1990).
Dream of Fair to Middling Women (1932), ed. Eoin O'Brien and Edith Fournier (Dublin: Black Cat Press, 1992).
Eleuthéria (Paris: Éditions de Minuit, 1995). *Eleuthéria* (London: Faber & Faber, 1996).

BIOGRAPHICAL STUDIES

Bair, Deirdre, *Samuel Beckett* (London: Jonathan Cape, 1978). First full-length biography.
Cronin, Anthony, *Samuel Beckett: The Last Modernist* (London: Harper Collins, 1996). Readable, good on Irish context.
Gordon, Lois, *The World of Samuel Beckett*. (New Haven and London: Yale University Press, 1996). Places Beckett's early life in its historical, social and cultural context.
Harmon, Maurice, (ed.), *No Author Better Served* (Cambridge, Mass.: Harvard University Press, 1998). Beckett's correspondence with his American director from the first American *Godot* till Schneider's death in 1984.
Knowlson, James, *Damned to Fame: A Life of Samuel Beckett* (London: Bloomsbury, 1996). As close as we have come to an authorized biography.

BIBLIOGRAPHIES

Admussen, Richard, *The Samuel Beckett Manuscripts: A Study* (Boston: GK Hall, 1978).
Cohn, Ruby, *A Beckett Canon* (Ann Arbor: University of Michigan Press, 2001). Exhaustive commentary on all known writings.
Davis, Robin J., *Samuel Beckett: Checklist and Index of his Published Works, 1967–76* (Stirling: NP, 1979). Checklist to Beckett's work.
Federman, Raymond, and Fletcher, John, *Samuel Beckett: His Works and His Critics* (Berkeley and Los Angeles: University of California Press, 1970). First bibliography.
——— ———, *Samuel Beckett: The Critical Heritage* (London: Routledge and Kegan Paul, 1979). A collection of responses, reviews and interviews.

CRITICAL WORKS

Abbott, H. Porter, *The Fiction of Samuel Beckett: Form and Effect* (Berkeley and Los Angeles: University of California Press, 1973). Stylistic account of the prose.

Acheson, James, and Arthur, Katerina (eds.), *Beckett's Later Fiction and Drama: Texts for Company* (Basingstoke: Macmillan, 1987). Excellent collection of criticism dealing with post-*Endgame* drama and post-Trilogy prose.

Alvarez, A., *Beckett* (London: Fontana, 1973). Includes drama and fiction up to *Not I*; reads Beckett's work as despairing recoil from conventional terrain of art.

Brienza, Susan, *Samuel Beckett's New Worlds: Style in Metafiction* (Norman, Okla., and London: University of Oklahoma Press, 1987). Influential reading of the late prose works.

Butler, Lance St J., and Davis, Robin J. (eds.), *Rethinking Beckett: A Collection of Critical Essays* (London: Macmillan, 1989). Strong collection of essays from a variety of critical perspectives.

Coe, Richard, *Samuel Beckett* (rev. edn., New York: Grove Press, 1968). Thematic.

Cohn, Ruby, *Samuel Beckett: The Comic Gamut* (New Brunswick: Rutgers University Press, 1962). Along with Kenner, the most influential of the early studies.

—— *Back to Beckett* (Princeton: Princeton University Press, 1973). Returns to texts, attempting to avoid overschematization of previous critical work.

—— *Samuel Beckett: A Collection of Criticism* (Basingstoke: Macmillan, 1987). Influential collection by many established Beckett scholars.

—— (ed.), *Samuel Beckett: Waiting for Godot: A Casebook* (Basingstoke: Macmillan Education, 1987). Draws together critical work with responses and reviews.

Connor, Steven, *Samuel Beckett: Repetition, Theory and Text* (Oxford: Basil Blackwell, 1988). Excellent theoretical discussion.

—— (ed.), *Waiting for Godot and Endgame* (Basingstoke: Macmillan, 1992). Strong collection of criticism, with a good overview on theoretical approaches of 1980s.

Debevec Henning, Sylvie, *Beckett's Critical Complicity: Carnival, Contestation and Tradition* (Lexington: University Press of Kentucky, 1988). Influential Bakhtinian reading of Beckett.

Dearlove, Judith, *Accommodating the Chaos: Samuel Beckett's Nonrelational Art* (North Carolina: Duke University Press, 1982). Deconstructive account of Beckett's work.

Esslin, Martin, *The Theatre of the Absurd* (London: Eyre and Spottiswoode, 1961). Includes influential reading of Beckett as existentialist dramatist.

—— (ed.), *Samuel Beckett: A Collection of Critical Essays* (Englewood Cliffs: Prentice Hall, 1965). First collection of critical essays devoted to Beckett's work.

Fitch, Brian T., *Beckett and Babel: An Investigation into the Status of the Bilingual Work* (Toronto, Buffalo, London: University of Toronto Press, 1988). Discussion of Beckett's bilingualism.

Fletcher, Beryl, Fletcher, John, Smith, Barry and Bachem, Walter, *A Student's Guide to the Plays of Samuel Beckett* (London: Faber & Faber, 1978). Introductory, aimed at undergraduate reader.

Fletcher, John, *Samuel Beckett's Art* (London: Chatto & Windus, 1967). Notable for early discussion of poetry, Beckett's criticism and his approach to French.

—— *The Novels of Samuel Beckett* (London: Chatto & Windus, 1964). Discusses Beckett's fiction in terms of his heroes' increasingly tenuous relations to the world.

—— and Spurling, John, *Beckett: A Study of his Plays* (London: Eyre Methuen, 1972). Introductory.

Friedman, Melvin J., *Samuel Beckett Now* (Chicago: University of Chicago Press, 1975). A re-evaluation of the critical approaches of the 1960s.

Gidal, Peter, *Understanding Beckett* (London: Macmillan, 1986). Post-structuralist and political account.

Gluck, Barbara, *Beckett and Joyce: Friendship and Fiction* (Lewisburg: Bucknell University Press, 1979). Re-evaluation of the relationship between Beckett and Joyce.

Gontarski, S. E., *The Intent of 'Undoing' in Samuel Beckett's Dramatic Texts* (Bloomington: Indiana University Press, 1985). Influential attempt to establish a common methodology behind plays.

Hale, Jane Alison, *The Broken Window: Beckett's Dramatic Perspective* (Indiana: Purdue University Press, 1987). Strong account of Beckett's theatre as disruptive of habitual structures of perception.

Harvey, Laurence, *Samuel Beckett: Poet and Critic* (Princeton: Princeton University Press, 1970). Only full-length discussion of SB's poetry, written with Beckett's help.

Hassan, Ihab, *The Literature of Silence: Henry Miller and Samuel Beckett* (New York: Knopf, 1967). One of the first readings of Beckett as postmodern.

Hesla, David H., *The Shape of Chaos: An Interpretation of the Art of Samuel Beckett* (Minneapolis: University of Minnesota Press, 1971). First entirely philosophical account of Beckett's work.

Hill, Leslie, *Beckett's Fiction: In Different Words* (Cambridge: Cambridge University Press, 1990). Excellent Derridean study of the fiction.

Kenner, Hugh, *Samuel Beckett* (New York: Grove, 1961). Reads Beckett as Cartesian artist. Thematic rather than chronological.

—— *A Reader's Guide to Samuel Beckett* (London: Thames & Hudson, 1973). Chronological study, biographical and historical.

Knowlson, James, and Pilling, John, *Frescoes of the Skull: The Later Prose and Drama of Samuel Beckett* (London: John Calder,1979). Deals with works from *Texts for Nothing* onward.

Locatelli, Carla, *Unwording the World: Samuel Beckett's Prose Works after the Nobel Prize* (Philadelphia: University of Pennsylvania Press, 1990). Poststructuralist account of the late prose.

127

McMullan, Anna, *Theatre on Trial: Samuel Beckett's Later Drama* (London: Routledge, 1993). Excellent study of the late drama.

Mercier, Vivian, *Beckett/Beckett* (New York: Oxford University Press, 1977). Account of Beckett's art through dialectical oppositions.

Moorjani, Angela, *Abysmal Games in the Novels of Samuel Beckett* (Chapel Hill, NC: University of North Carolina Press, 1982). Influential reading of Beckett's fiction.

Morot-Sir, Edouard, Harper, Howard, and McMillan, Dougald, *Samuel Beckett: The Art of Rhetoric* (Chapel Hill, NC: University of North Carolina Press, 1976). Contains important essay by Morot-Sir reviewing history of Cartesian analysis in Beckett.

Pilling, John, *Samuel Beckett* (London and Boston: Routledge & Kegan Paul, 1976). Comprehensive discussion of influences, literary and philosophical. Sections on intellectual, cultural and literary background.

—— (ed.), *The Cambridge Companion to Samuel Beckett* (Cambridge: Cambridge University Press, 1994). Strong collection of essays covering Beckett's entire œuvre.

—— *Beckett before Godot* (Cambridge: Cambridge University Press, 1997). Detailed consideration of Beckett's early writing.

Robinson, Michael, *The Long Sonata of the Dead* (London: Hart-Davis, 1970). Study of Beckett's work as heroic existential quest.

Trezise, Thomas, *Into the Breach: Samuel Beckett and the Ends of Literature* (Princeton: Princeton University Press, 1990). Standard postmodern reading of Beckett.

Webb, Eugene, *Samuel Beckett: A Study of his Novels* (London: P. Owen, 1970). Reads Beckett's fiction in terms of his response to Dante, Descartes and Proust.

—— *The Plays of Samuel Beckett* (Seattle: University of Washington Press, 1972). Companion piece to his study of the novels, sequential study of plays in tradition of the absurd.

Worth, Katherine (ed.), *Beckett the Shape Changer* (London and Boston: Routledge & Kegan Paul, 1975). Essay collection concentrating on formal innovation.

—— *The Irish Drama of Europe from Yeats to Beckett* (London and New Jersey: Athlone Press, 1978). Relates SB's work to twentieth-century Irish writing in its European context.

Zilliacus, Clas, *Beckett and Broadcasting: A Study of the Works of Samuel Beckett for and in Radio and Television* (Abo: Abo Akademi, 1976). Remains only full-length study of this area of SB's work.

The two main journals dealing with Beckett are the *Journal of Beckett Studies* and *Samuel Beckett Today/Aujourd'hui*. The Samuel Beckett Society also publishes *The Beckett Circle*.

128

Index

130

Lightning Source UK Ltd.
Milton Keynes UK
10 December 2009

147309UK00001B/18/A

9 780746 308578